Business
BENCHMARK

Advanced
Higher

D1696667

Personal Study Book

Guy Brook-Hart

CAMBRIDGE UNIVERSITY PRESS
Cambridge, New York, Melbourne, Madrid, Cape Town,
Singapore, São Paulo, Delhi, Tokyo, Mexico City

Cambridge University Press
The Edinburgh Building, Cambridge CB2 8RU, UK

www.cambridge.org
Information on this title: www.cambridge.org/9780521672979

First published 2007
6th printing 2011

Printed in the United Kingdom at the University Press, Cambridge

A catalogue record for this publication is available from the British Library

ISBN 978-0-521-67294-8 Student's Book with CD-ROM BULATS edition
ISBN 978-0-521-67661-8 BULATS edition Audio Cassettes (2)
ISBN 978-0-521-67662-5 BULATS edition Audio CDs (2)
ISBN 978-0-521-67295-5 Student's Book BEC Higher edition
ISBN 978-0-521-67298-6 BEC Higher edition Audio Cassettes (2)
ISBN 978-0-521-67299-3 BEC Higher edition Audio CDs (2)
ISBN 978-0-521-67296-2 Teacher's Resource Book
ISBN 978-0-521-67297-9 Personal Study Book

Author's note

To the student

This Personal Study Book provides you with two pages of extra exercises and activities for each unit of the Student's Book. The exercises and activities are designed to reinforce what you have studied and they cover vocabulary, grammar, reading and writing.

It is a good idea to do the work in each unit of the Personal Study Book *after* you have finished the unit in the Student's Book. This will help you to remember things you have studied. You will need to write your answers in your notebook. Do the exercises regularly while the things you have studied in the Student's Book are still fresh in your memory.

Check your answers by looking in the key on pages 70–80. If you are not sure why an answer in the key is correct, ask your teacher to explain.

When you do the writing exercises, you can compare your answer with a sample answer in the answer key. If your teacher agrees, you can give him/her your answer to correct.

If you are preparing for the Cambridge ESOL BEC Higher exam or the BULATS test, many of the exercises are designed to give you exam practice.

The Personal Study Book also contains a Word list. These are words and phrases from the units and recording transcripts of the Student's Book which may be unfamiliar to you, or difficult to understand. When you find new words in the Student's Book, always try to guess the meaning first from the context. Keep a list of new vocabulary in your notebook. In general, use the Word list to check the meanings later, not while you are doing the exercises in the Student's Book.

Acknowledgements

The authors and publishers are grateful to the following for permission to reproduce copyright material. While every effort has been made, it has not always been possible to identify the sources of all the material used, or to trace the copyright holders. If any omissions are brought to our notice, we will be happy to include the appropriate acknowledgements on reprinting.

p. 13: AskMen.com for the text 'Advice for organising meetings', taken from the website www.AskMen.com. Used by permission of AskMen.com, a division of IGN Entertainment, a unit of Fox Interactive Media, Inc.; p. 15: LOMA for the text 'Measuring customer satisfaction'. Reprinted from James Huffman and Tom Moorman *Resource*, October 2002, pp. 34–35. Copyright © 2002 LOMA (Life Office Management Association, Inc.). All rights reserved. Reprinted with permission from the publisher. This material may not be reproduced without the express written consent of LOMA. For more information about LOMA and its educational programs, visit www.loma.org; p. 21: Decision News Media for the text 'Nestlé in Thailand' published on www.dairyreporter.com, 11 June 2004 on which the charts are based; p. 31: Kyodo News International, Inc. for the text 'Nissan sets record', *The Japan Times*, 3 February 2006. © All rights reserved. Used by permission of Kyodo News International, Inc.; p. 33: *The Guardian* for the text 'Gadget shop folds' by Mark Tran, 14 April 2005, p. 47: text 'The Day Chocolate Company' by Sophi Tranchell, 22 November 2005. Copyright Guardian Newspapers Limited, 2005; pp. 38–39: *Workforce Management* for the text 'Where paying dues delivers' by Douglas P. Shuit, May 2005. Used by permission of Workforce Management, Crain Communications, Inc.; p. 43: *The Economist* for the text 'Industrial Metamorphosis' 29 September 2005. © The Economist Newspaper Limited; pp. 54–69: various of the definitions are from the *Cambridge Advanced Learner's Dictionary*, www.dictionary.cambridge.org.

Illustrations: Hart McLeod; **Design and layout:** Hart McLeod; **Project management:** Jane Coates; **Edited by:** Catriona Watson-Brown; **Production controller:** Gemma Wilkins; **Senior commissioning editor:** Charlotte Adams; **Publishing manager:** Sally Searby

Contents

UNIT 1 Corporate culture

Vocabulary

1 Match the words on the left (1–7) with the words on the right (a–g) to make phrasal verbs with the definitions given in brackets.

1 get — a down to (*is essentially*)
2 come — b ahead (*make progress*)
3 boil   c out (*begin*)
4 start   d over (*discuss thoroughly*)
5 stick   e to (*follow/obey*)
6 talk   f up (*arrive*)
7 turn   g up with (*produce ideas/solutions*)

2 Complete this text using the phrasal verbs from Exercise 1 in the correct form.

> 1 *Getting ahead*, or making progress, in my company really 2 ....
> working hard and 3 .... the guidelines laid down by management. The
> company I work for doesn't encourage originality, especially at the beginning
> when you 4 .... On the other hand, they're very supportive and they are
> always ready to 5 .... problems and help you 6 .... a solution. One thing
> you mustn't do, however, is 7 .... to meetings late, as good timekeeping is
> considered to be very important!

3 Write a similar paragraph about the place where you work or study. Use as many of the phrasal verbs from Exercise 1 as you can.

4 Match words and phrases from the two columns to make typical collocations or expressions.

1 dress — a of directors
2 bottom   b competition
3 cut-throat   c line
4 board   d code
5 make   e or swim
6 market   f race
7 rat   g share
8 red   h someone redundant
9 sink   i tape

5 Complete these sentences using the collocations/expressions from Exercise 4 in the correct form.

1 When your company tells you what sort of clothes you should wear to work, they have a ..dress code.. .

2 When the rivalry between different companies is very fierce, we talk about ....

3 When the amount a company sells rises faster than its competitors, we can say that they are increasing their ....

4 When workers compete with each other in a very stressful way to get to the top of their companies or professions, we say they are part of the ....

5 When you lose your job because of market forces, you have been ....

6 In a company where you're not given much help learning your job, the situation is often called '.....................'.

7 Bureaucratic paperwork is frequently referred to as '.....................'.

8 The top executives who make the important strategic decisions for a company sit on the ....

9 The final profit or loss of a company is often referred to as 'the ....'.

Grammar

Join these sentences using defining or non-defining relative clauses. If necessary, look at Grammar workshop 1 on page 26 of the Student's Book.

1 We use a yardstick to measure our success. The yardstick is customer satisfaction.

....The yardstick (which/that) we use to measure our success is....
....customer satisfaction.....

2 Our production process has been undergoing some streamlining. This should have a beneficial effect on our bottom line.

3 We will be receiving a visit from the chairman of the board next week. You saw his recent email.

4 Our company is situated in a quiet area. The area is right in the heart of the country.

5 They've just given me a bonus. The bonus is the equivalent of three months' salary!

6 In our company, problem-solving takes place at informal get-togethers. During the get-togethers everyone sits down on some sofas near the coffee machine.

7 Some companies have strict dress codes. Their corporate culture is quite traditional.

8 You set me some goals. Those goals are impossible to achieve.

Leaders and managers

Vocabulary

1 In each of these sentences there is a mistake in the spelling. Underline the misspelt words and write them correctly.

1 It's important for managers to pay <u>atention</u> to the nitty-gritty.   *attention*
2 His main responsability is to produce financial forecasts.   ....
3 We hold annual apraisal interviews in September.   ....
4 We're expecting a foreign delagation to visit headquarters soon.   ....
5 The underlaying cause of our poor performance is productivity.   ....
6 Branson has reinforced his billionnaire, jet-setting reputation.   ....
7 Leaders need innovative ideas to make a sucess of their companies.   ....
8 Few businesses have been promoted so aggressively.   ....

2 Choose the best word, A, B, C or D, to complete these sentences.

1 Branson aims to ..*turn*.. his empire into the most respected brand in the world.
  A put   (**B** turn)   **C** set   **D** get
2 Generally ...... , I think being a high-profile person has its advantages.
  A talking   **B** saying   **C** speaking   **D** expressing
3 Advertising costs enormous ...... of money these days.
  A amounts   **B** masses   **C** numbers   **D** loads
4 Last week, he announced that he was ...... up a domestic airline in India.
  A putting   **B** making   **C** doing   **D** setting
5 The costs of promoting the business will be extremely high in advertising ....
  A ways   **B** methods   **C** terms   **D** types
6 If you like people, you can ...... out the best in them.
  A get   **B** bring   **C** pull   **D** make
7 Branson ...... enormous value on time-management skills.
  A places   **B** gives   **C** serves   **D** pours
8 He ...... a third of his time on trouble-shooting.
  A passes   **B** gives   **C** makes   **D** spends
9 He has ...... up several businesses from scratch.
  A built   **B** made   **C** put   **D** run
10 He has to be good at helping people ...... the businesses and then stepping back.
  A do   **B** play   **C** run   **D** make

3 Complete these sentences with collocations with *management*. If necessary, look again at page 17 in the Student's Book.

1 She never seems to be able to meet her deadlines; I think we should send her on a ..time-management.. course.

2 We've had a number of defective products returned. It might be a good idea to overhaul our .... systems.

3 When the factory caught fire, our .... procedures were severely put to the test.

4 Some of our leading products could do with better .... in order to maintain their market positions.

5 By outsourcing non-core activities, we should reduce our exposure to a downturn in the market. I call that good ....

6 His job is more a consultative role within the organisation. He's not involved in the direct .... of workers.

7 You don't want to be stuck in .... for too long. You should be looking to move into senior management by the time you are 45 or 50.

4 Complete these sentences with prepositions.

1 This is my first time ...in.... a management role.

2 If you believe .... the capabilities of your staff, they will probably perform better.

3 He really has a hands- .... approach to managing the department.

4 He's keen to get .... and do his job well.

5 In his appraisal interview, they agreed .... a strategy for giving him more empowerment.

6 The woman he works .... is very ready to delegate responsibility.

7 It is important to be given responsibility .... what you are doing.

8 How have management techniques changed .... the last ten years?

9 How can you get the best .... your workers?

10 He works best when he's .... a manageable amount of pressure.

Grammar

Complete these sentences with *as* or *like*.

1 ...Like. our competitors, we're having difficulty keeping our prices low.

2 .... we foresaw, oil prices soared in the second half of the year.

3 .... you may have realised, our French partners are not entirely happy with our performance.

4 I wouldn't like to have another crisis .... the one we had last week.

5 In my job .... a management consultant, I'm often called in to see why businesses are failing.

6 Last year's profits were at almost the same level .... the year before's.

7 She thinks we could outsource a number of activities, ... computer maintenance and office cleaning.

8 There are several cities in South America where I wouldn't mind being posted, such .... Rio de Janeiro or Santiago.

Internal communications

Reading

Complete this email by writing one word in each space.

Delete	Reply	Reply All	Forward	Compose	Mailboxes	Get Mail	Junk

Hello Francesca,

Thanks very much **1** ...for.... the report. I read it last night and was most impressed **2** .... the content and by **3** .... punctual you have been in submitting it. **4** .... I mentioned to you last week, I shall be circulating it to other departmental heads for their comments and reactions in **5** .... next few days.

There are just one **6** .... two points I would like to **7** .... up with you: firstly, you say in section 3 that 'a considerable increase **8** .... budget will be necessary if we are **9** .... meet these targets'. Perhaps you were not aware that a 35% budget increase was approved by the finance director last week, and I think that should cover the extra costs **10** .... have been forecast.

The **11** .... point is the timescale: you suggest starting the new project by the end of the year at the **12** .... , but I think, given the fact that we are extremely short-staffed, next May would be more realistic **13** .... a starting date.

14 .... you would like to discuss this with me, or make the changes before the report is circulated, give me a ring.

Again, many thanks for an excellent piece of work.

Angela

Vocabulary

> **Prefixes** *over–* **and** *under–*
>
> *Over–* often means 'in excess': *I think we have a tendency to overdo things* (i.e. do too much). The opposites of such words are usually made with *under–*: *I'm afraid you've seriously underestimated the time required for this project.*

1 Complete these sentences with a word with the prefix *over–*.

1 When you have too much work, you are .overworked. .

2 When a product's price is too high, it is ....

3 A worker who management values too highly is ....

4 An office which has too many staff is ....

5 When difficulties have been estimated to be greater than they really are, they have been ....

6 Someone with too many qualifications for the job they're doing is ....

7 A project which has received too many funds is ....

8 Someone who is reacting too strongly to something is ....

2 What are the opposites of the answers to Exercise 1?

3 Complete the sentences below with a verb from the box in the correct form and with the correct prefix, *over–* or *under–*.

| charge | prepare | rate | sleep | ~~use~~ |

1 Could staff please use the photocopier less? At the moment, it's being seriously ..overused.. – remember: this is supposed to be a paperless office!
2 He seriously .... his presentation and had far too much material.
3 I don't think .... is a good excuse for arriving late for work.
4 I think people tend to .... his abilities as a manager; he's far better than you think.
5 This invoice shows that we've been .... by nearly $90. Can you phone them and ask for a refund?

4 Match these common business words (1–6) with their meanings (a–f).

1 overbearing (*Unit 2*)   a charge less than (your competitors)
2 overdraw   b debit more from an account than you have credited
3 overheads   c dominating
4 oversee   d routine fixed costs
5 overwhelming (*Unit 1*)   e supervise
6 undercut   f very large number/amount of

5 Complete these sentences with the words from Exercise 4 in the correct form.

1 I'm not directly involved in the project, but I do have to .oversee. the expenditure to make sure it doesn't go over budget.
2 It can be very frustrating if you have an .... boss who doesn't allow you space to grow.
3 The .... majority of our staff would welcome a more flexible timetable.
4 The bank sent him a letter of warning because his account was .... for the third time.
5 We will have to become more efficient and reduce our prices because we're being seriously .... by foreign competitors.
6 We will have to control our .... more tightly if we are going to increase our profits.

Chairing meetings

Vocabulary

1 Complete the sentences below with one of the words in the box to make expressions a chair might say at or after a meeting.

| ahead | just | latecomers | meeting | miss | poor | run | ~~timescale~~ | timing |

1 Can I just ask your ideas on what the timescale should be for this project?
2 If you think you're going to have trouble in .... the deadline, please make sure everyone is aware of it in good time.
3 In future, could .... please come in as quietly as possible so as not to disrupt proceedings?
4 In general, this committee's work is very good. My only complaint is about some members' .... timekeeping.
5 Now, I know some of you have other engagements directly afterwards, so I won't let this meeting .... over time.
6 Phew! I thought I was going to be late because of the traffic, but I see I'm .... in time to get the meeting under way on schedule.
7 As you know, we're all working really hard because we have a deadline looming which we don't want to ....
8 We've made more progress than I expected, and I think we'll finish the work well .... of time.
9 Yes, I agree, it's a question that had to be asked, but it was just bad .... asking it at such a sensitive moment.

2 Match these words (1–9) with their definitions (a–i).

1 outcome — a a summary of the main facts
2 outline b amount produced
3 outlook c beginning
4 outperform d do better than others
5 output e expressing strong opinions very directly
6 outsell f likely future situation
7 outset g not yet paid, solved or done *or* excellent
8 outspoken h result
9 outstanding i sell more than another product

3 Complete these sentences with the words from Exercise 2 in the correct form.

1 I don't want you to summarise the whole report, just give us an outline of your main conclusions.
2 As a management consultant, I have to be .... in certain circumstances, otherwise firms don't take on board my recommendations.

3 It was understood from the .... that a renewal of your contract was linked to satisfactory results, so you shouldn't be surprised that we're letting you go.
4 The .... from our factory in Düsseldorf is disappointing, and if productivity doesn't pick up, we'll have to close it down.
5 The economic .... is grim: high inflation, rising interest rates and unemployment, so perhaps it's not a good time to invest.
6 Their new range of cars are at the moment .... their closest rivals by two to one, and this is doing wonders for their market share.
7 We're in better shape to confront the recession because we've consistently .... our main competitors.
8 What was the .... of your discussions with Charlie? Will he do the job?
9 You have three invoices .... Please settle them as soon as possible as this is affecting our cashflow situation.

Reading

Choose the best word, A, B, C or D, to fill each space in this text.

Advice for organising meetings

Prepare an agenda and 1 ..*set*.. objectives for the meeting. Share this information with the other attendees well in advance and invite them to add agenda 2 ...... in the days or weeks before the meeting. If it's not possible to 3 ...... the agenda in advance, at least review it at the start of your meeting. Start on time and do not repeat everything for latecomers unless it is absolutely essential. Use a flip chart or whiteboard to write down valid issues that arise to be discussed later, so as to avoid 4 ...... the planned order of business. After planning your objectives, determine who should attend. If a heated argument breaks out, stand up and recap both sides, allowing each faction to feel heard and understood. As the meeting leader, remember that someone needs veto 5 ...... to cut through debates and bring back order, and that responsibility falls squarely on your shoulders. At the close of any meeting, ensure that you 6 ...... recap the major decisions reached and the next steps planned. 7 ...... the date and time of the next meeting, if one is necessary. Organise a well-planned session where the participants feel that the subject is worthwhile, their 8 ...... is valued, and their needs are 9 ...... , and you'll not only conduct a successful meeting, you'll 10 ...... your corporate morale and image.

1 **A** set	**B** form	**C** ascertain	**D** ensure
2 **A** things	**B** lists	**C** items	**D** bullets
3 **A** send	**B** circulate	**C** pass	**D** post
4 **A** agitating	**B** disrupting	**C** disorganising	**D** confusing
5 **A** rule	**B** force	**C** strength	**D** power
6 **A** shortly	**B** briefly	**C** curtly	**D** abruptly
7 **A** Assure	**B** Approve	**C** Ratify	**D** Confirm
8 **A** output	**B** input	**C** outcome	**D** outset
9 **A** dealt	**B** looked	**C** cared	**D** met
10 **A** rise	**B** soar	**C** boost	**D** rocket

Customer relationships

Vocabulary

1 Complete this table with as many words as possible. (Many of the words can be found in Unit 5 of the Student's Book.)

Noun	Verb	Adjective
1 *assistant* *assistance*	assist	
2	advertise	
3	4	reliable
rival, rivalry	5	6
7	retain	
profit, profitability	8	9
strategy		10
11	satisfy	12
13		loyal
14	organise	15
16	acquire	
17	expand	
apology	18	19
20	cancel	

2 Form 11 compound nouns by combining a word from box A with a word from box B. You can check your answers by looking back at the five extracts on page 31 in your Student's Book.

Example: *business strategy*

A

business
buying
customer
human
management
product
profit
savings

B

account	policies
care	resources
development	retention
habits	services
manager	strategy
margins	

3 Complete these sentences with compound nouns from Exercise 2.

1 Information technology allows us to build up detailed information about individual customers' ..buying habits.. .

2 The costs of .... are much lower than the costs of recruiting new customers.

3 Companies have to reorientate themselves by switching .... from product management to CRM.

4 Looking after customers, which is often known as ...., generates costs and is therefore often perceived as eating into ....

Reading

Choose the best option, A, B, C or D, to complete this text.

Measuring customer satisfaction

Delivering effective customer service is a **1** ..goal.. shared by virtually every successful company, whether it's a small retail outlet in your neighbourhood, your favourite restaurant, or a multibillion-dollar insurance company. Why do these companies **2** ...... on service? Because excellent customer service **3** ...... with a great product will lead to **4** ...... profitability.

Everyone **5** ...... good service when they experience it, or so we would like to think. Yet for many people, good service may simply be expected and thus taken for **6** .... What stands out in the customer's mind is excellent service that **7** ...... expectations and poor or inferior service that fails to **8** ...... them. Put simply, the greater the satisfaction of the customer, the higher the profits. Unfortunately, simply measuring customer satisfaction is not enough. It is necessary to understand the factors that **9** ...... it and work on these factors to attain and maintain the **10** ...... levels.

Satisfied customers of an insurance company will **11** ...... to pay premiums, buy more products and cost **12** ...... to service. And satisfied customers will usually tell other people of their experience. On the other hand, unhappy customers may tell more people about their experience than if they were satisfied.

1 A wish	B hope	C goal	D desire
2 A look	B focus	C emphasise	D check
3 A connected	B joined	C related	D combined
4 A raised	B increased	C soared	D boosted
5 A understands	B notices	C recognises	D identifies
6 A granted	B made	C done	D given
7 A passes	B overtakes	C outdoes	D exceeds
8 A encounter	B meet	C comply	D answer
9 A drive	B push	C involve	D include
10 A wanted	B wished	C hoped	D desired
11 A go on	B carry on	C continue	D stay
12 A lower	B smaller	C fewer	D less

Competitive advantage

Vocabulary

1 Choose the best word, A, B, C or D, to complete these sentences.

1 Bryson Ltd is a company with a ..proven.. track record.
   A shown   **B** demonstrated   **C** proven   **D** displayed

2 Only by using effective marketing ...... can you attract the customers you need.
   A notes   **B** strategies   **C** communications   **D** forms

3 We have to constantly innovate in order to be one ...... ahead of the competition.
   A step   **B** position   **C** place   **D** leap

4 By keeping our prices low and our quality high, we aim to give our customers ...... for money.
   A worth   **B** cheapness   **C** value   **D** bargains

5 Samsons got involved in a price war, and with prices so low, they were unable to ...... their costs.
   A cope   **B** handle   **C** deal with   **D** cover

6 We try to charge the highest price the market will ...... without losing market share.
   A take   **B** bear   **C** suffer   **D** accept

7 A high price often ...... quality to customers who have no other way of assessing it.
   A signals   **B** shows   **C** demonstrates   **D** proves

8 You have to give customers good service from the ...... , otherwise you won't keep them.
   A outlook   **B** outcome   **C** outlay   **D** outset

9 What we require is ...... from our staff in order to beat our rivals.
   A commitment   **B** compromise   **C** devotion   **D** trust

10 They put the job out to ...... in order to find the best contractor for the project.
   A bid   **B** offer   **C** negotiation   **D** tender

2 Complete this text using the phrasal verbs from the box.

| bid for | come up with | come to | go about |
| go for | put together | team up with | work out |

We **1** ..go about.. looking for work by looking in the *Journal of the European Union*. Then, if we see something that catches our attention and we decide to **2** .... it, we'll often **3** .... a firm of architects, and together we **4** .... a plan and **5** .... a design for the project. We then have to **6** .... the work, which means we have to **7** .... how much it will all cost – in other words, add up all the items and see what it will **8** .... – and then offer a price.

3 Complete this crossword.

Across

3 If you can't ...... your costs, you won't make a profit.
4 We would like to ...... a tender for this work.
5 Companies who don't take care of their customers go out of ......
6 You need to ...... more time to your customer relationships.

Down

1 Once you've managed to ...... a relationship with a customer, you must maintain it.
2 It can be quite difficult to ...... the value of a project before you start.
3 We don't try to ...... on price – instead we offer higher quality.

Grammar

Complete these sentences with the verbs in brackets in the correct conditional form.

1 If we .hadn't recruited. (*recruit*) an IT specialist last year, the company .wouldn't have bought. (*buy*) such an up-to-date computer system.
2 If they .... (*introduce*) a flexible working system, I wouldn't have to travel during the rush hour.
3 I don't work at head office, but if I .... (*do*), I .... (*find*) it very convenient.
4 We .... (*easily afford*) that state-of-the-art machine if we .... (*budget*) for it during the last financial year.
5 I .... (*learn*) a lot about the Spanish market if they .... (*send*) me to work for their subsidiary in Salamanca, but I don't think they will.
6 We lost the contract because of your negligence. If you .... (*devote*) more time to customer relationships, we .... (*get*) the work.
7 I .... (*bid*) for a contract unless I .... (*think*) we could make a profit on it.

A proposal

Vocabulary

1 Complete these sentences using the phrases in the box. One phrase is used more than once.

and at the same time
apart from
furthermore
in connection with
in response to
in turn
since
therefore
~~while~~

1 ....While...... they've increased their market share, this hasn't as yet led to increased profits.

2 The company has had to reduce prices .... increased competition from overseas.

3 We've received a number of angry letters .... our poor levels of customer service.

4 None of our departments seems to be able to keep within budget .... the finance department.

5 I wonder, ... you're going to be in Kiev on Tuesday, if you could deliver this package while you're there?

6 There was a postal strike which led to a delay in mail deliveries. This, ... , led to a delay in invoice payments.

7 The project is at a highly sensitive opening stage. I would ask you .... to treat everything to do with it as highly confidential.

8 .... our Polish subsidiaries, none of our other concerns in Eastern Europe is making a profit yet.

9 This has been an interesting .... a highly productive meeting.

10 Your invoice arrived three weeks late. .... , when it arrived we found it contained major errors.

2 Match words from box A and box B to form as many compound nouns as you can.

Example: account number

A

account	export
company	key
computing	negotiating
contact	office
entrance	operating

B

car	instructions
error	manager
furniture	number
hall	skills
holder	worker

Grammar

Change these sentences into the passive, starting with the words given.

1 We should have replaced the old computer system three years ago.
The old computer system _should have been replaced three years ago_ .

2 Nobody said anything at the meeting about a change of supplier.
Nothing …

3 They might need to revise the component specifications.
   The component specifications …
4 They haven't reported any losses in the last ten months.
   No …
5 The government may bring new regulations into effect next year.
   New government regulations …
6 They must have allocated funds for this in their budget.
   Funds …
7 This is the first time we have marketed this product in the USA.
   This product …
8 We'd never have recruited Simon if he hadn't been so brilliant at his interview.
   Simon …

Reading

There is one extra word in most lines of this proposal. However, some lines are
correct. Write the extra word on the right. If a line is correct, put a tick (✓).

Introduction
The purpose of this proposal is to suggest ways in which the current system   1 ✓
of recruitment can be improved and made more effective ~~one~~.   2 one

Current system
At present, all of vacant posts are advertised in local and regional   3
newspapers. Prospective candidates are asked to submit to an application   4
and curriculum vitae, and they are then short-listed and after invited to   5
interview. All short-listed candidates are being required to supply references   6
from some current or recent employers, or, in the case of first-time workers,   7
from tutors or head teachers.   8

Drawbacks of current system
Advertising is more expensive, and the time spent by human resources staff   9
in screening potential candidates increases significantly adds to this cost.   10
Also, while doing interviews are an essential part of the recruitment process,   11
too many of the people who are invited to interview are not of the required   12
quality. This also represents a cost in the terms of time.   13

A new recruitment system
I propose that, in future, jobs which are not open for high-level managers or   14
technical experts should have be recruited using the services of a recruitment   15
agency. This in effect would involve outsourcing a large part of the screening   16
process and they should ensure that we are only presented with good   17
candidates at the final interview stage. This system would save time for human   18
resources because: 19
• advertisements would not need to be written up   20
• applications would still not need processing.   21

Conclusion and recommendation
I foresee no drawbacks with this change in our system and I recommend that   22
we proceed to the next step, which it is to identify a suitable recruitment   23
agency and employ them on a trial basis for to see if they can provide the   24
service we require.   25

Presenting at meetings

Vocabulary

1 Match these words (1–11) with their definitions (a–k). All the words occurred in the three texts on pages 42 and 43 of the Student's Book.

1	allocate	a	amount a company sells as a percentage of the total possible sales in a market
2	gain ground on	b	amount of money available for people to buy things
3	boost	c	become more popular or accepted than (a competitor)
4	capitalise on	d	changes or variations
5	fluctuations	e	develop or grow quickly
6	shelf life	f	give a share of a total amount
7	per capita	g	having a lot of money
8	penetration	h	increase
9	burgeon	i	length of time that a product can be kept in a shop before it becomes too old
10	affluence	j	per person
11	spending power	k	use a situation advantageously

2 Complete these sentences using the words from Exercise 1 in the correct form.

1 Twenty-five per cent of our marketing budget has been .allocated. for promotions in South-East Asia.

2 Income .... has risen over the last ten years by more than 50%.

3 Since many of our perishable goods have a short .... , it's difficult for us to reach more remote parts of the country.

4 The market for hand-held electronic goods is .... , and we stand to make major profits in the future.

5 The stock market is very unstable at the moment, with wild .... in share prices.

6 They .... sales last autumn by undercutting other major players.

7 They managed to launch their ice-creams successfully by .... their reputation as a quality frozen-food producer.

8 We hope, over the next couple of years, to deepen .... of the market and reach at least 25% of consumers.

9 We hope that a vigorous marketing campaign together with some new product lines will allow us to .... our main rivals.

10 With growing .... within the country, people are able to buy more, and this increased .... means that we can charge higher prices and sell higher-quality products.

Writing

Study the charts below and, if necessary, look again at the transcript for Track 15 in the Student's Book. Write what you might say if you were giving a short informal presentation about the Thai ice-cream market at a business meeting. If possible, use some of the phrases from the box.

along with	and another thing	apparently	as to the second
but anyway	in terms of	so you can imagine that	to be exact
to give you a bit more background		you can see that	

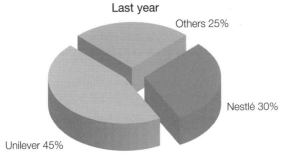

Thailand: ice-cream market share
Last year

Others 25%

Nestlé 30%

Unilever 45%

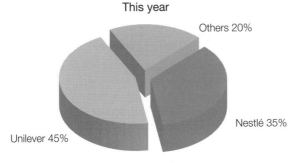

Thailand: ice-cream market share
This year

Others 20%

Nestlé 35%

Unilever 45%

Grammar

Correct the mistake in each of these questions.

1 Could you tell me how do you intend to boost sales?
   <u>Could you tell me how you intend to boost sales?</u>
2 I wonder how much will it cost to launch our products in the Far East.
3 I will be grateful if you could tell me what our projected market penetration is for next year.
4 Can you to tell me how much spending power is forecast to increase in Thailand?
5 Do you happen to know what is the shelf life of our rivals' products?

Advertising and customers

Vocabulary

1 Complete these sentences with the phrases from the box. There is one phrase you will not need.

boost sales
brand awareness
~~brand building~~
market share
product launch

1 Anything which a company does to make a brand better known and better regarded is called .brand building. .

2 Companies advertise obviously to sell products but also to raise .... , so that more people just know a brand exists.

3 A typical marketing ploy (or tactic) is to advertise in advance of a .... so as to create expectation, and then when it comes on the market, it sells well.

4 An important measure of how well a brand is doing in comparison to its competitors is .... , and this is something companies try to increase by advertising.

2 Match these forms of advertising (1–5) with the place you would expect to see them (a–e).

1 advertising hoardings
2 banner ads
3 classified ads
4 point-of-sale displays
5 product endorsements

a in a shop
b in a newspaper
c in the street
d on a website
e on television / at the cinema

3 Choose the best option, A, B, C or D, to complete these sentences.

1 Could you remind. me to write a cheque for the technician before I leave?
   A recall   B remember   C remind   D review

2 Their publicity campaign failed to ...... much interest in the general public.
   A raise   B rise   C arouse   D provoke

3 We certainly couldn't have got the new project off the ground without the consultancy's ...... advice.
   A valueless   B priceless   C worthless   D invaluable

4 In just a matter of a few years, their brand has become a ...... name.
   A home   B housing   C domestic   D household

5 Our customers' buying ...... have changed radically in the last ten years.
   A customs   B habits   C trends   D behaviour

6 The technology allows researchers to establish a link between people's ...... to advertisements and their buying patterns.
   A experience   B exposure   C appreciation   D contact

7 People are increasingly able to ...... the advertising from television and the Internet so that it no longer interrupts their activities.
   A filter out   B phase out   C shut off   D cut up

8 Kendalls' recent price cuts have ...... sales and increased their market share.
   A soared   B pushed   C boomed   D boosted

Reading

Complete each gap in this email with a suitable word.

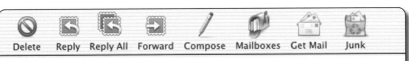

Delete | Reply | Reply All | Forward | Compose | Mailboxes | Get Mail | Junk

Maria,
Here's a summary of our discussion yesterday and the decisions we **1** ..*came*.. to.
- We discussed **2** ...... advertising medium would be **3** ...... suitable for our B2B
  software products and decided that **4** ...... addition to our web-based advertising, we
  should also **5** ...... use of the trade journals which companies of the type we supply
  software to are **6** ...... to read.
- We agreed that you would contact a couple of advertising agencies, who would
  7 ...... up with proposals and sample designs for our ads. We would also ask them to
  identify suitable journals and **8** ...... us an estimate of the total cost of running the
  campaign.
- We agreed that measuring the effectiveness of the advertising will be relatively easy
  to **9** .... Any customers acquired **10** ...... the course of the campaign or shortly
  11 ...... will be asked how they heard **12** ...... us – by word of mouth or through our
  advertising. We will then, in due course, be **13** ...... to measure **14** ...... effective the
  advertising has been in relation to the money we have invested **15** ...... it.
Carlo

Grammar

Complete this letter by putting the adverbs in brackets in the correct position in
each sentence. In many cases, more than one answer is possible.

Hello Bill,

1 I'm writing to report on the effectiveness of the advertising we've been doing.
  (*briefly / recently / just*)
  I'm just writing briefly to report on the effectiveness of the
  advertising we've been doing recently.
2 Sales have been slow, despite our campaign. (*disappointingly / unfortunately*)
3 I think this is because the advertisements do not state what we do. (*frankly /
  clearly enough*)
4 They do state that we are electrical engineers. They don't state what our
  speciality is, i.e. repairing electric motors. (*curiously / however*)
5 I was looking at the page and I notice that it looks similar to advertisements
  for our rivals, Manning Ltd. (*surprisingly / also / just an hour ago*)
6 People phone us up asking if we are Manning Ltd. (*quite often / indeed*)
7 I believe that we need to continue advertising. (*firmly*)
8 We need to improve the appearance of our advertisements. (*urgently / however*)
9 I'm meeting a friend from an advertising agency, and he'll come up with
  something which works. (*more effectively / tomorrow / hopefully*)

Best wishes
Mike

Vocabulary

1 Complete this crossword.

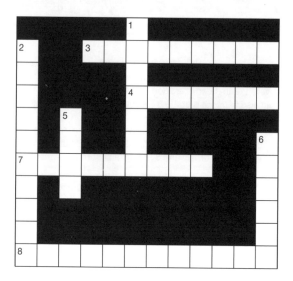

Across

3 Some programs allow Internet users to .... advertisements they don't want to see. (6, 3)

4 It is very unusual these days for a company not to have a .... (7)

7 .... are a type of publicity you find on some websites. (6, 3)

8 Use a .... to find websites connected with a subject. (6, 6)

Down

1 A .... is a program which allows you to access the Internet. (7)

2 Some adverts appear automatically in .... when you visit a website. (3-2, 5)

5 You can sometimes click on a .... which will connect you to another website.

6 Doing business .... is one of the fastest-growing commercial areas. (6)

2 Complete these sentences using the correct form of the verbs *make* or *do*.

1 The advertisement ..makes. a number of claims for the product which have little basis in reality.

2 A website has become an essential part of .... business with consumers.

3 You shouldn't expect to .... a huge profit in the first year.

4 You won't .... a sale unless the customer can actually see and touch the vehicle.

5 Many car buyers want to feel they are .... a deal when they buy a car, so be prepared to offer them a discount.

6 For several years, many dotcom companies didn't .... any money from their activities.

7 An advertisement won't .... an impression unless it is humorous or surprising.

8 I've been .... the accounts all morning and I still haven't finished.

Reading

Study this chart and read the report below. In most lines of the report, there is an extra word. However, some lines are correct. Cross out the extra words and write them on the right. Where a line is correct, put a tick (✓).

Processed meat companies: Advertising and sales, five years ago – now

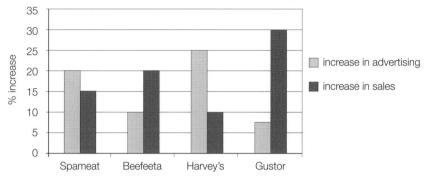

This report summarises the relationship between the increase in ~~its~~   1   its
spending on advertising over the last five years time and the rise in sales   2
over the same period for four processed-meat companies. The company   3
which it has increased its advertising spending the most was Harvey's,   4
which has raised up its budget by 25%. However, its sales have gone up by   5
only 10%. Gustor, on the other hand, has only spent 8% more than on   6
advertising over this period, but was managed a 30% increase in sales. In a   7
more modest way, Beefeeta's performance has been similar to, with a 10%   8
increase in spending and a 20% rise in sales. In a contrast, Spameat's   9
advertising appears to have been less successful, because although they   10
have spent 20% more on advertising, their sales have only just risen by   11
15%. However, it should be pointed out that these figures represent   12
percentage changes rather than the global figures.   13

Writing

Study this chart and write a brief report describing the information in it.

Supermarkets by market share and advertising spend last year

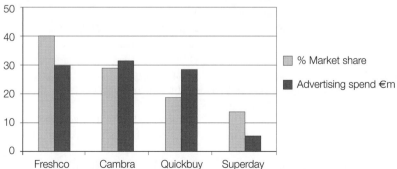

Vocabulary

1 Complete these sentences using words or phrases from the box.

prospect	sales pitch
sales volume	selling point

1 Frank delivered his usual ………. when he went to visit a new customer, but he made the mistake of not really listening to what the customer wanted.

2 He's out visiting a ………. at the moment. Let's hope he makes a sale and gets us closer to our monthly target.

3 I should think we shift about 10,000 of these every month, which is a pretty good ………. really.

4 This product's main ………. is its extraordinary versatility; it works well in almost all atmospheric conditions.

2 Choose the best option, A, B, C or D, to complete these sentences.

This type of exercise can be a quick way to learn quite a lot of new vocabulary: check you know the meanings of all the alternatives and why the wrong answers are wrong.

1 When you're selling B2B (business to business), you'll never get a new customer unless you can persuade them that buying your product will produce favourable outcomes.. for them.
   A outcomes   **B** outlays   **C** outlets   **D** outgoings

2 We've been working hard at …… customer service by providing better facilities.
   A advancing   **B** bettering   **C** enhancing   **D** reforming

3 You'll be a great salesperson one day; you've just got to get the …… and that's something which doesn't just come with training. You need experience, too.
   A ability   **B** knowledge   **C** grasp   **D** knack

4 Buying your product would represent a considerable …… for our firm, Mr Simmons. How could we justify it?
   A outgoing   **B** outlay   **C** output   **D** outplacement

5 He's one of our super-salesmen who travel the world on a(n) …… account and manage to land contract after contract.
   A diet   **B** cost   **C** payment   **D** expense

6 To be successful in sales, your clients need to trust you, and to do that you need total …… .
   A faith   **B** trustfulness   **C** integrity   **D** faithfulness

7 An investigation into why the company was unable to pay its debts …… that they had been overtrading for several months.
   A disclosed   **B** revealed   **C** uncovered   **D** displayed

8 I think we've been rather clever; we've …… the competition by slashing prices by 20%.
   A cut down   **B** cut back   **C** cut off   **D** undercut

Grammar

Put the verbs in brackets into the most suitable form: present perfect simple or present perfect continuous.

1 No, I'm not new to this profession – I've been doing (*do*) it for more than 30 years.

2 I .... (*not see*) you all morning. .... you .... (*work*) on the invoices?

3 I still .... (*not finish*) the report you asked me to write. .... you .... (*wait*) for it?

4 I'm glad to say that sales .... (*increase*) this year, although we still .... (*not achieve*) our target.

5 I'm not surprised I'm looking tired. I .... (*work*) 12 hours a day all week, but it .... (*be*) worth it because I .... (*sell*) £2 million worth of equipment.

6 Sorry I didn't get in touch with you earlier. I .... (*mean*) to call you all day, but I .... (*have*) so many phone calls myself that I just .... (*not manage*) to get round to it.

7 We .... (*share*) an office while Vanessa has hers redecorated.

8 I .... (*tell*) you countless times that he'll never buy anything from you unless you visit him in person.

9 They .... (*try*) to find the solution to this glitch in R&D, but they .... (*not come*) up with anything yet.

10 It .... (*take*) some time for our company to come to terms with the new market situation, but I think we .... (*take*) it on board at last.

Writing

Use words in the box to write a short report about the line graph below.

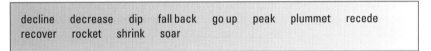

| decline | decrease | dip | fall back | go up | peak | plummet | recede |
| recover | rocket | shrink | soar | | | | |

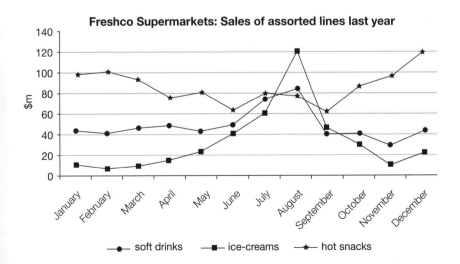

Freshco Supermarkets: Sales of assorted lines last year

— soft drinks — ice-creams — hot snacks

The sales pitch

Vocabulary

Choose the best option, A, B, C or D, to complete these sentences.

1 Many large companies will avoid outsourcing to unknown small companies because they are risk- .ọvẹṛsẹ. .
   A unwilling   B unprepared   C uncooperative   (D averse)

2 Who is ...... in the event of an accident?
   A liable   B blamed   C faulty   D responsive

3 It's proving hard to ...... the precise person responsible for the auditing mistake. I wish we knew who it was.
   A track   B track down   C monitor   D turn up

4 We need to get a good firm of solicitors ...... if we're going to produce a credible proposal for these people.
   A on track   B online   C on time   D on board

5 When the new computer system is ...... , we should be able to process data in a much more integrated way.
   A up and coming   B up and running   C in the running   D on board

6 We have a rigorous ...... process to weed out unsuitable candidates.
   A filter   B choosing   C screening   D selective

Grammar

1 A salesperson is cold-calling a company to sell space in a private car park near the company's office. Put the words in these questions in the correct order.

1 about mind business? I Do ask you a few you questions if your

2 can has? tell how First, me employees your you many company

3 staff be in work thinking Would that of most I your come right by to car?

4 And last do problems your one work? staff parking question: have at

5 in for be interested employees? parking Would spaces your you leasing

2 Rewrite these sentences as cleft sentences starting with the word(s) given.

1 I certainly don't intend to give all the work to you.
   The last thing ...I intend to do is (to) give all the work to you...............

2 I didn't expect such a generous bonus.
   What ....

3 I just said I was a bit doubtful.
   All ....

4 I was really interested in the product because of its low price.
   It was ....

5 My staff do nothing but complain all day.
   All my staff ....

6 The managing director was responsible for the mix-up.
   It was ....
7 They outsourced all their sales to an outside agency.
   What they ....
8 We definitely don't want a visit from head office.
   The last thing ....
9 We need a completely new sales strategy.
   What ....
10 You just have to sign this form.
   All ....

Reading

1 Read the email below following up a cold call. What is the purpose of each paragraph?

2 Complete the email by writing one word in each space.

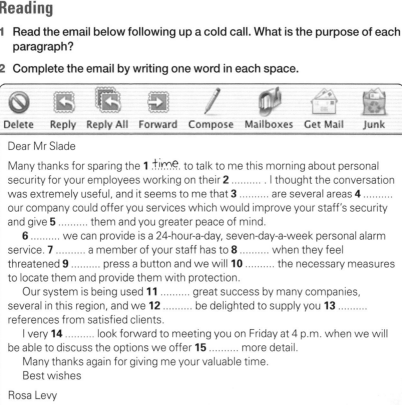

Delete   Reply   Reply All   Forward   Compose   Mailboxes   Get Mail   Junk

Dear Mr Slade

Many thanks for sparing the **1** time. to talk to me this morning about personal security for your employees working on their **2** .... I thought the conversation was extremely useful, and it seems to me that **3** .... are several areas **4** .... our company could offer you services which would improve your staff's security and give **5** .... them and you greater peace of mind.

   6 .... we can provide is a 24-hour-a-day, seven-day-a-week personal alarm service. **7** .... a member of your staff has to **8** .... when they feel threatened **9** .... press a button and we will **10** .... the necessary measures to locate them and provide them with protection.

   Our system is being used **11** .... great success by many companies, several in this region, and we **12** .... be delighted to supply you **13** .... references from satisfied clients.

   I very **14** .... look forward to meeting you on Friday at 4 p.m. when we will be able to discuss the options we offer **15** .... more detail.

   Many thanks again for giving me your valuable time.

   Best wishes

Rosa Levy

Writing

Imagine you have cold-called a prospective customer about a product or service your company provides and the person has shown interest and agreed to meet you. Write a follow-up email to the phone call in which you:

- thank the person for talking to you and refer to your telephone conversation
- give a summary of the product or service and how it will benefit your prospect
- mention your many satisfied customers and refer to the meeting you have arranged at a future date.

13 Forecasts and results

Vocabulary

1 Complete these sentences using the expressions or phrasal verbs from the box. Where necessary, put the verbs into the correct form.

1 After weeks of arguing, they managed to *talk someone into* taking the job, although she didn't really want to relocate.
2 He .... the offer of promotion because he didn't want to relocate to Alaska.
3 How do you .... making sales forecasts? Do you just pull a number out of the air, or are you more methodical?
4 I'm afraid the meeting .... expectations; we expected to solve everything and we managed to solve almost nothing.
5 I'm quite confident our investment will .... as long as interest rates remain low.
6 We had a visit from an .... young executive from Boston, who suggested a joint venture to us.
7 Who would want to buy that design? It's so strange I doubt if it will ever ....

> catch on
> fall short of
> go about
> pay off
> ~~talk someone into~~
> turn down
> up-and-coming

2 Complete the financial statement below using the headings from the box.

> Depreciation   Goodwill   Overdraft   Premises   Pre-tax profits
> Profit and loss for the period   Shareholders' equity
> Stock   Total fixed assets   ~~Turnover~~

Pennings Plc. Financial Statement

Profit-and-loss account

	€m
1 Turnover	220
Cost of sales	(120)
2	(30)
Operating cost	(20)
Operating profit	70
Interest payable	(25)
3	45
Tax	(12)
Profit after tax	33
Dividends	(20)
4	13
Retained earnings	175
5	188

Balance sheet

	€m
Cash in bank	100
6	12
Debtors	21
Total current assets	**133**
7	50
Equipment	21
8	**71**
9	43
Total assets	**247**
Creditors	(17)
10	(42)
Total current liabilities	**(59)**
Total assets less liabilities	**188**

Grammar

Each of these conditional sentences contains one mistake with a verb. Find and correct them.

1 I'm sure we won't do this, but if we reduce our overheads, our cashflow would be much healthier.

I'm sure we won't do this, but if we reduced our overheads, our
cashflow would be much healthier.

2 Our products are really attractive, and if they had caught on, we'll make a fortune.

3 I wouldn't have managed to talk him into working for me if he wasn't turned down for that job last year.

4 The company would go bankrupt last year if it hadn't been given an overdraft by the bank at the last minute.

5 If we didn't lay off 20% of the workforce, we won't be able to keep our heads above water – it's really necessary that we do so.

6 Redlands wouldn't have introduced a flexible working system if the workers wouldn't have demanded it.

Reading

Complete this newspaper report with words and phrases from the box.

> fixed assets   forecast   net profit
> ~~operating profit~~   pre-tax profit
> turnover   volume

Nissan sets record

Nissan Motor Co. said Thursday its group **1** .operating.profit.. for the first nine months of the year through March 31 rose 3.1 per cent from a year before to a record 631.16 billion yen, chiefly due to brisk demand in Japan, North America and Europe.

Group **2** .... in the reporting period climbed 11.4 per cent to 6.79 trillion yen, the automaker said. In terms of **3** .... , sales leaped 10.0 per cent to 2,653,648 vehicles. **4** .... ,

however, slipped 1.1 per cent to 605.47 billion yen and **5** .... dipped 2.0 per cent to 365.69 billion yen due primarily to losses related to the introduction of a pension plan and the value depreciation of **6** .... the car maker said.

The company kept intact its earlier **7** .... for its earnings in the year ending this March, with pre-tax profit projected at 860 billion yen, up from 855.70 billion yen in fiscal 2004.

from *The Japan Times*

Writing

You work for the finance team at Presto Bearings. Your CEO has asked you to write a brief report summarising the financial performance of the company last year.

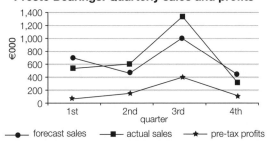

Presto Bearings: Quarterly sales and profits

€000: 1,400 / 1,200 / 1,000 / 800 / 600 / 400 / 200 / 0 — 1st, 2nd, 3rd, 4th quarter

—●— forecast sales   —■— actual sales   —★— pre-tax profits

14 Financing the arts

Grammar

1 Complete these sentences by putting the verb in brackets into the correct form (infinitive or –ing form).

1 ..Being. (be) Head of PR involves constantly .... (have) to find new ways of .... (present) the company to the public.

2 Our main competitor keeps .... (bring) out new products, none of them very cheap.

3 He avoided .... (speak) to her all through the conference.

4 He'll never agree .... (put) up money for a business venture like that.

5 I couldn't resist .... (have) a flutter on the stock exchange.

6 I wouldn't dare .... (start) a new business in the present economic climate.

7 If you decide .... (back) a company like that, you risk .... (lose) all your money very soon.

8 She strode into reception demanding .... (see) the managing director!

9 The company has failed .... (make) a profit for the third year running.

10 They attempted .... (reduce) overheads, but with no success.

11 We aim .... (be) a global brand within five years.

12 We couldn't afford .... (invest) in new equipment.

13 Well, Bill, let's celebrate your .... (survive) your first 12 months with our firm.

14 When we launch the new company, how long will it be before we can expect .... (break) even?

2 In some of these sentences, the writer has made a mistake by writing an infinitive where there should be an –ing form, or vice versa. However, some sentences are correct. Correct the mistakes. Where a sentence is correct, put a tick (✓).

1 Barry has arranged ~~holding~~ to hold the presentation in the boardroom at five.

2 AFG have reported losing more than €30m in the third quarter.

3 Are you intending visiting the July trade fair in Munich?

4 Can I suggest taking a break, as we can't reach a decision quickly?

5 Do you happen knowing the interest rate in Japan at the moment?

6 Don't hesitate phoning me if you have any questions.

7 He denied to buy the shares using inside knowledge.

8 It's outrageous. They're threatening to withdraw their backing if we don't promise giving them 50% of the profits.

9 Our customers tend to be middle-aged rather than young.

10 She's very capable and really deserves to be given more responsibility.

11 The new accountant has proved to be totally incompetent.

12 They've decided to postpone implementing their plans until the situation becomes clearer.

13 Would you consider to break into the Indian market as a way of expanding sales?

Reading

Choose the best word, A, B, C or D, to complete this article.

Gadget Shop folds

The Gadget Shop today lost its battle for survival, 1 .putting. 620 people out of 2 .... , after two potential bidders walked away. The administrator of the 3 .... chain, PKF, said the potential buyers were 4 .... about the weak level of retail spending and the 5 .... of stock. The 45 outlets of the company, which sells pocket camcorders, handheld MP3s, DVD players and toys, will shut over the next four weeks.

Bryan Jackson, the joint administrator, said it was disappointing that a suitable offer did not 6 .... 'The potential buyers we 7 .... to all expressed concern that they could not clearly 8 .... how long it would take them to 9 .... , purchase and make available suitable stock,' he said. 'Furthermore, this is a quiet time of year for this business sector, a sector that is not 10 .... well overall.' Closing-down sales would now take place to 11 .... as much money as possible for creditors, he added. 'We will aim to sell individual or groups of stores, the company name and its successful website.'

The Gadget Shop was placed in administration after debts climbed to £3m and sales 12 .... over Christmas. The executive chairman, Chris Gorman, and the Scottish entrepreneur Tom Hunter, and the chief executive and founder, Jonathan Elvidge, who held a combined share-holding of 60%, were keen on 13 .... of the chain.

Established in 1991, the Gadget Shop was finding it difficult to 14 .... against department stores and toy shops offering similar products at a time when consumers are 15 .... their belts.

from the *Guardian*

	A	B	C	D
1	making	placing	putting	getting
2	work	job	employment	occupation
3	broke	failed	bankrupt	folded
4	annoyed	concerned	critical	upset
5	supply	offer	provision	loan
6	appear	materialise	arise	form
7	spoke	agreed	called	informed
8	work	know	deduce	estimate
9	encounter	source	identify	attract
10	working	acting	achieving	performing
11	regain	renew	retract	recoup
12	lowered	slumped	reduced	cut
13	disposing	selling	auctioning	parting
14	rival	struggle	combat	compete
15	attaching	closing	tightening	fastening

15 Late payers

Vocabulary

1 Complete these sentences using the words in the box plus one of these prefixes: *un–*, *out–*, *over–*, *up–*.

authorised	come	draft	due	due	front
goings	lay	lets	market	~~trading~~	valued

1 Continuing to operate when you have little prospect of paying your creditors or your employees is known as .overtrading and it's illegal.

2 Delivery of the consignment we ordered is three days ...., and this is playing havoc with our production schedules.

3 Fortunately, we've gained a temporary reprieve from the cashflow problem, as the bank has granted us an extension to our ....

4 Frankly, I wouldn't buy that factory site for that price. I think it's grossly ....

5 I'm a bit short of cash at the moment, as I've had so many .... this month.

6 The product is available in a wide range of retail .... throughout the city.

7 They've moved their products .... to take into account changes in consumer tastes.

8 We have decided not to take disciplinary action as a result of your .... absence from work – but next time we will!

9 We want you to enjoy working for us, so let us know if we're putting you under .... pressure, and we'll see what we can do to relieve it.

10 What was the .... of your negotiations with the Canadian company yesterday?

11 Investing in a new computer system would represent a considerable .... for a small firm like ours.

12 They insist on us making an initial payment .... before they supply us with any of the goods.

2 Combine words from box A with words from box B to form business collocations. In some cases, more than one combination is possible.

A

bookkeeping	cash	credit
overdue	punitive	root
time	unauthorised	undue

B

bank charges	cause	constraints
limit	overdraft	payment
pressure	skills	worthiness

3 Complete these sentences with collocations from Exercise 2. (You won't be able to use all the collocations you formed.)

1 The new suppliers require us to make a .cash payment. for the first consignment.

2 The position would suit someone with experience in office administration and advanced ....

3 You will have to pay .... if you exceed the .... on your overdraft.
4 The high prices we have to pay for raw materials is a .... of our industry's lack of competitiveness.
5 The .... mean it is unlikely that we will submit a tender for this particular contract. After all, the deadline for submissions is the end of this month.
6 The bank sent me a pretty stiff letter after I ran up an ....
7 I hope you don't think we're putting you under .... to complete this project.
8 You should check new customers' .... before supplying them with goods.

Reading

Read this email to a business friend. Choose the more informal option for each pair of phrases in *italics*.

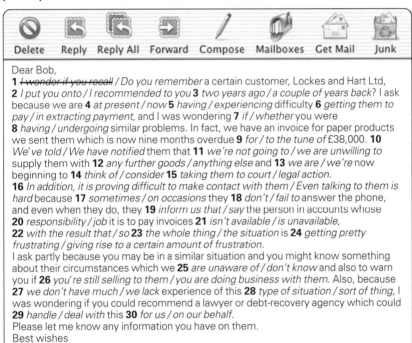

Dear Bob,
1 ~~I wonder if you recall~~ / *Do you remember* a certain customer, Lockes and Hart Ltd,
2 *I put you onto* / *I recommended to you* **3** *two years ago* / *a couple of years back*? I ask because we are **4** *at present* / *now* **5** *having* / *experiencing* difficulty **6** *getting them to pay* / *in extracting payment*, and I was wondering **7** *if* / *whether* you were **8** *having* / *undergoing* similar problems. In fact, we have an invoice for paper products we sent them which is now nine months overdue **9** *for* / *to the tune of* £38,000. **10** *We've told* / *We have notified* them that **11** *we're not going to* / *we are unwilling to* supply them with **12** *any further goods* / *anything else* and **13** *we are* / *we're* now beginning to **14** *think of* / *consider* **15** *taking them to court* / *legal action*.
16 *In addition, it is proving difficult to make contact with them* / *Even talking to them is hard* because **17** *sometimes* / *on occasions* they **18** *don't* / *fail to* answer the phone, and even when they do, they **19** *inform us that* / *say* the person in accounts whose **20** *responsibility* / *job* it is to pay invoices **21** *isn't available* / *is unavailable*, **22** *with the result that* / *so* **23** *the whole thing* / *the situation* is **24** *getting pretty frustrating* / *giving rise to a certain amount of frustration*.
I ask partly because you may be in a similar situation and you might know something about their circumstances which we **25** *are unaware of* / *don't know* and also to warn you if **26** *you're still selling to them* / *you are doing business with them*. Also, because **27** *we don't have much* / *we lack* experience of this **28** *type of situation* / *sort of thing*, I was wondering if you could recommend a lawyer or debt-recovery agency which could **29** *handle* / *deal with* this **30** *for us* / *on our behalf*.
Please let me know any information you have on them.
Best wishes
Angela

Writing

Your company has been experiencing problems with a supplier and your manager has asked you to write to a business friend in another company which uses the same supplier in order to:

- find out if their company is experiencing similar problems
- ask for information regarding the supplier
- warn them about the problems they might have
- ask for advice about dealing with the situation.

Write 200–250 words.

16 Negotiating a lease

Vocabulary

Complete these negotiating phrases with one of the words or phrases from the box.

1 Well, it's .not ideal. , but I think we could do it.
2 We'll give you that increase, ... it's part of a two-year agreement.
3 So, the first thing we have .... is the price. We want £60 per unit. How do you feel about this?
4 Perhaps we'd better .... business. Would you like to state your requirements first?
5 OK. So let's just .... the points of our agreement again.
6 Now, let's see what we've got to discuss. I've .... a few things here. What about you?
7 Let's see if I've got this .... You want us to pay £500 .... and the rest in a month's time.
8 I've drawn up a rough .... for discussions. Is there anything you'd like to add?
9 .... we paid the price you're asking. Would you be prepared to give us a .... if we place an order of more than 1,000 units?

> agenda
> as long as
> discount
> get down to
> go over
> jotted down
> ~~not ideal~~
> on our list
> straight
> suppose
> upfront

Grammar

Complete the sentences below using one of the alternatives to *if* from the box. In most sentences, more than one answer is possible; you can use each phrase more than once.

> as long as   imagine   on condition (that)   on the one condition (that)
> provided (that)   providing (that)   suppose   supposing   unless

1 .Suppose/Supposing/Imagine. we don't reach agreement. How will your company survive?
2 We're prepared to pay the asking price, ... that you undertake to give us the very highest quality.
3 We won't take any further action .... you authorise us to do so.
4 We won't be able to continue paying that price .... interest rates come down by at least two points.
5 We should be able to meet our financial targets .... the stock market holds steady.
6 So, ... we hold the next meeting in Beijing. How would that suit you?
7 My client has stipulated that he will accept your offer .... that he can pay in dollars, otherwise the deal is off.
8 I'll agree to your request for a day's leave .... you promise to do the work later in the month.

9   Anyway, ... we were able to source these parts more cheaply elsewhere. Where would you find another customer as reliable as we've been over the years?

10   .... we said we didn't have the production capacity. Who could you source similar quality goods from instead of us? No one and you know it!

Reading

This email from a personnel manager to other management colleagues contains one extra word in most lines. However, some lines are correct. Write the extra words on the right. Where a line is correct, put a tick (✓).

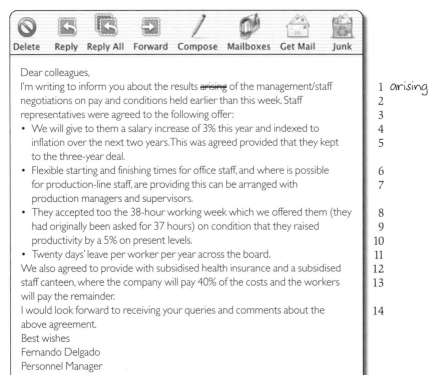

| | Delete | Reply | Reply All | Forward | Compose | Mailboxes | Get Mail | Junk |

Dear colleagues,

I'm writing to inform you about the results ~~arising~~ of the management/staff   1 arising
negotiations on pay and conditions held earlier than this week. Staff   2
representatives were agreed to the following offer: 3
• We will give to them a salary increase of 3% this year and indexed to   4
  inflation over the next two years. This was agreed provided that they kept   5
  to the three-year deal.
• Flexible starting and finishing times for office staff, and where is possible   6
  for production-line staff, are providing this can be arranged with   7
  production managers and supervisors.
• They accepted too the 38-hour working week which we offered them (they   8
  had originally been asked for 37 hours) on condition that they raised   9
  productivity by a 5% on present levels.   10
• Twenty days' leave per worker per year across the board.   11
We also agreed to provide with subsidised health insurance and a subsidised   12
staff canteen, where the company will pay 40% of the costs and the workers   13
will pay the remainder.
I would look forward to receiving your queries and comments about the   14
above agreement.
Best wishes
Fernando Delgado
Personnel Manager

Writing

You have received the email above from Fernando Delgado. However, there are some points which you think are unclear. Write an email to Fernando pointing out what you think is unclear and asking for clarification. Use the list on the right to help you, if necessary.

Salary increase to start from which month?

What is the 'three-year deal'?

More details required about flexible working times

How will productivity (for office staff) be measured and by whom?

17 Workplace atmosphere

Vocabulary

Choose the best option, A, B, C or D, to complete these sentences.

1 Companies where staff morale is high tend to ..*outperform*.. their competitors.

   A outdo   **B** outgrow   **C** outperform   **D** outrun

2 An effective form of motivation is through ...... -group recognition.

   A peer   **B** equal   **C** level   **D** same

3 In order to be able to maintain ...... , you need to be able to attract the best staff.

   A rivalry   **B** competitiveness   **C** opposition   **D** hostility

4 Making people redundant should be the last ...... for companies in difficulties.

   A resource   **B** result   **C** report   **D** resort

5 During the last economic downturn, they had to ...... about 10% of the workforce.

   A send off   **B** put off   **C** drop off   **D** lay off

6 Workers need to receive ...... pay or they will soon move on.

   A same   **B** comparative   **C** level   **D** competitive

Grammar

1 Complete this text using the words from the box. You will not need one of the words.

do	he	her	herself	its	~~one~~
one	such	there	this	those	
what	where	which	whose	why	

UPS

1 ..*One*.. of Lea Soupata's favorite photographs captures Jim Casey, the founder of United Parcel Service. 2 .... is standing in 3 .... of the company's offices in Massachusetts, staring into the distance.

Reflecting on 4 .... image, the company's senior vice-president of people programs says, "He is just standing 5 .... , probably thinking, 'Gee, it's a long way from Seattle,'" 6 .... he founded the company in 1907.

After rising to the top of the world's fourth-largest employer, Soupata might just as well look at her roots in a working-class neighborhood of New York and say of 7 .... , "Gee, it's a long way from Queens."

Separating 8 .... from UPS is almost impossible. She's been at the company for 36 years, in jobs ranging from truck driver to member of the board of directors of a firm 9 .... time-tested organizational style dates back nearly a century to the days of foot and bicycle messengers.

Workforce management is 10 .... UPS is all about, from 11 .... liberal employee benefits program to its highly structured system of internal mobility. As its 384,000-member workforce holds on to the distinction of being the largest delivery and transportation company in the world, **12** .... traditions are being tested as never before.

Today, it is fighting to stay ahead of archrival FedEx, as well as two government-assisted mail-delivery monopolies, the U.S. Postal Service and Germany's Deutsche Post World Net, the German postal service **13** .... owns the delivery company DHL. Among the key players helping UPS to **14** .... so in the face of **15** .... stiff competition is Soupata, the daughter of a working-class Greek immigrant family.

from Workforce Management

2 Rewrite these sentences using a suitable reference device to avoid repetition.

1 I'm director of R&D, and as director of R&D, I'm in charge of all new product development.

   I'm director of R+D, and as such, I'm in charge of all new product development

2 The date of our next meeting has been postponed, and the postponement will mean that no decision will be taken for at least a month.

3 They were advised to place an advertisement in all major national newspapers, and they placed an advertisement in major national newspapers.

4 Monique and Michelle did an MBA together at London University. Now Monique works for Tesco and Michelle works for Asda, two of the largest supermarket chains in Britain.

5 Kostas and Dimitriou were our representatives in Greece. Both Kostas and Dimitriou were made redundant when we closed our operation in Greece.

6 Marcel is the finance director. Marcel is the director who took the decision – and it was a difficult decision.

7 He's asked me to take over the Berlin office, and I've agreed to take over the Berlin office.

8 Sven has been discussing the problem with Franz, but Sven doesn't agree with Franz.

3 Rewrite these sentences using the words and phrases given in brackets.

1 Repetitive work often causes boredom and demotivation amongst workers. (*gives rise*)

   Repetitive work often gives rise to boredom and demotivation amongst workers

2 Companies sometimes cut prices because of pressure from rivals. (*causes companies to*)

3 We are having cashflow problems as a result of some late payers. (*given rise*)

4 The bad winter weather has been causing delivery problems. (*arisen*)

5 We laid off some workers because their productivity was low. (*led*)

6 Tiredness occasionally causes workplace accidents. (*occasional consequence*)

7 He sometimes loses his temper when under excessive stress. (*causes him to*)

8 Over-reliance on computer systems is a major cause of breakdowns in customer relations. (*major consequence*)

18 The workforce of the future

Vocabulary

1 Complete these sentences using the words or phrases from the box.

freelancer
project manager
shop-floor
union rep
~~temp~~
white-collar

1 I think we'll have to take on a ..temp. while Olga is on maternity leave.
2 He started at the bottom as a .... worker in our factory in Bratislava, before becoming a manager a year or two later.
3 We'll have to negotiate these changes with the workers' elected .... before implementing them.
4 He left the company some time ago to become a .... and now he does consultancy work for a number of different companies.
5 This construction project is much more complicated than we first thought; perhaps we should hire a .... to run it.
6 Since we outsourced nearly all our manufacturing requirements, we employ almost no blue-collar workers. Nearly all our employees are .... workers, working in our offices throughout Europe.

2 Match these phrases (1–6) with their definitions (a–f).

1 self-controlled
2 self-disciplined
3 self-employed
4 self-explanatory
5 self-financing
6 self-sufficient

a able to provide everything you need for yourself without the help of other people
b easily understood from the information already given and not needing further explanation
c having strong control over your emotions and actions
d not working for an employer, but finding work for yourself or having your own business
e paid for only by the money that an activity itself produces
f the ability to make yourself do things you know you should do, even when you do not want to

3 Complete these sentences with the phrases from Exercise 2.

1 As a presenter, he is very ...self-controlled... ; although I know he finds it very stressful, he rarely shows any sign of nerves.
2 He was .... for years before finally becoming a member of staff.
3 Hopefully our staff in our new Lisbon office will be completely .... within a month or two, and we won't have to give them any more training.
4 I think these instructions are more or less .... , so we shouldn't have much difficulty in following them.
5 The beauty of the new project is that it's .... , so we won't have to look for funds from elsewhere.
6 There's a lot of dull routine work to be completed, so we'd better be .... or we won't finish it before the holidays.

4 Complete these sentences with the phrases from the box.

1 She needs to change jobs every three or four years or else she feels she is .$stuck in a rut$. .

2 It may not be very profitable just now, but .... I'm sure it's going to be a big money-spinner.

3 I'm exhausted because I've been .... since six o'clock this morning.

4 He's just getting work-experience at the moment, but he hopes to .... full-time as soon as he finishes his university degree.

5 As long as I'm paid .... for the job, I'll be happy to do the work.

> get taken on
> in the long run
> on the go
> ~~stuck in a rut~~
> the going rate

5 Complete these sentences with the adjectives from the box.

1 Although her work is ..underpaid.. , she feels she is getting experience which she'll find useful in the future.

2 He's working as a public relations officer for a highly .... fashion house in Milan.

3 It's no good working with .... machinery. It just wastes your time.

4 Reduced loyalty to the company is a(n) .... feature of modern workplaces.

5 The .... majority of our workforce would like us to introduce a private health scheme.

6 The chairman of SoftChip has made the .... announcement that he is going to take a 50% reduction in salary.

7 The Stock Exchange was the scene of .... activity this morning as brokers rushed to buy shares in the new company.

8 There's every chance, with a .... job market, that all these young people will find work.

> booming
> frenetic
> obsolete
> overwhelming
> pervasive
> prestigious
> ~~underpaid~~
> unprecedented

6 Complete this memo with a suitable word in each space.

Memo

To: Sonia

The following is a brief report, **1** .as. requested, on our experiences of job sharing during the last three months.

Reasons

As you will recall, we asked for the opportunity to share jobs in order to allow both of us to attend **2** ...... pressing family commitments while at the same time **3** ...... able to maintain our positions within the company and part of our incomes.

Arrangement

We **4** ...... worked 20 hours a week as opposed **5** ...... a full-time job of 38 hours a week and received half our original salaries. **6** ...... our hourly rate of pay was reduced, our tax liabilities were also lower, **7** ...... we did not miss out financially. We had a

half-hour overlap in shifts **8** ...... served as a hand-over period.

Results

Since only a small part of our job involves direct contact **9** ...... customers, the arrangement worked well. We were able to plan and share **10** ...... most of our workload at the beginning of the week. We were both motivated to ensure that the scheme was a success, and so **11** ...... our partner for one reason or another **12** ...... behind with his/her work, we were willing to take **13** ...... and ensure that deadlines were **14** ....

Recommendation

We would strongly recommend this scheme to be continued and **15** ...... available to other employees who request it.

19 Productivity

Vocabulary

Choose the best option, A, B, C or D, to complete these sentences.

1 They have almost entirely automated the ..*assembly*.. line, which has led to spectacular reductions in labour costs.
   A construction   B output   C assembly   D manufacture
2 The new installations have allowed us to expand our production .... by 50%.
   A ability   B capacity   C capability   D volume
3 We run a lean manufacturing process, which means we avoid .... components before we need them.
   A keeping   B holding   C collecting   D stockpiling
4 We now have about 50 more workers on our .... , in spite of our productivity drive.
   A staff list   B payroll   C salary bill   D wage packet
5 Magro Toys has .... workers by automating the plant.
   A dropped   B cut down   C decreased   D shed
6 Most staff savings have been achieved by natural .... , such as early retirement and workers leaving voluntarily to take up employment elsewhere.
   A loss   B dropping   C wastage   D cutting

Grammar

1 Complete these sentences with the correct form of the modal verb and main verb in brackets.

1 I have a strong suspicion that someone *may have sabotaged* (*may/sabotage*) the assembly line, and that's why it stopped.
2 The figures just don't look right to me. Someone .... (*must/make*) a mistake.
3 The photocopier .... (*can't/break*) down again. We only had it mended last week.
4 If the photocopier has broken down again, it's because you .... (*must/use*) the wrong paper.
5 I'm told you haven't received the package yet, and I'm afraid I .... (*might/send*) it to the wrong address.
6 I have a suspicion that our clients .... (*may/speak*) to our competitors, and that's why they haven't put in an order yet.
7 He .... (*must/read*) my report by now because I sent it over a week ago.
8 They're so late! I suppose they .... (*could/get*) lost coming here, though I did send them a map.
9 They .... (*should/make*) your order up right now – I sent it through half an hour ago.
10 No, they .... (*can't/forget*) to do it. I reminded them just recently.

2 Complete these sentences in any way you like.

1 My assistant hasn't come to work today. She could …
2 It's a completely new computer system. It can't …
3 We gave you an enormous budget. You can't …
4 What a fantastic result to the negotiation! You must …
5 I don't know why they've dropped the case. Their lawyers may …
6 He's one of the top international experts on the subject, so he should …

Reading

Choose the best word, A, B, C or D, to complete this article from
The Economist.

Since, contrary to conventional wisdom, manufacturing **1** .output. has been growing strongly not **2** …… , the fall in employment in America and **3** …… should be seen as a good thing. It does not represent a dramatic **4** …… shift of production from developed economies to emerging economies. Instead, it largely reflects rapid productivity **5** …… . And because unemployment levels in most developed economies have not increased during the past decade, even though manufacturing jobs have been lost, it would appear that most laid-off factory workers have found new jobs.

Deindustrialisation – the **6** …… of industrial jobs – is popularly perceived as a symptom of economic decline. On the contrary, it is a natural **7** …… of economic development. As a country gets richer, it is **8** …… that a smaller proportion of workers will be needed in manufacturing. The first reason is that households need only so many cars, fridges or microwaves, so as they become richer, they tend to spend a bigger **9** …… of their income on services, such as holidays, health and education, rather than on goods.

Second, it is much easier to automate manufacturing than services, **10** …… men by machines. Faster productivity growth than in services means that manufacturing needs fewer workers. In turn, as workers move into more productive **11** …… , this gives a boost to overall productivity and hence living **12** …… .

1	**A** outlay	**B** output	**C** outlet	**D** outset
2	**A** reducing	**B** cutting	**C** declining	**D** lowering
3	**A** elsewhere	**B** wherever	**C** anywhere	**D** throughout
4	**A** utter	**B** extreme	**C** overwhelming	**D** wholesale
5	**A** rise	**B** increase	**C** growth	**D** surge
6	**A** slippage	**B** stoppage	**C** shortage	**D** shrinkage
7	**A** jump	**B** step	**C** pace	**D** phase
8	**A** unacceptable	**B** unstoppable	**C** inevitable	**D** unthinkable
9	**A** lump	**B** bulk	**C** chunk	**D** chop
10	**A** changing	**B** switching	**C** replacing	**D** substituting
11	**A** regions	**B** areas	**C** places	**D** zones
12	**A** standards	**B** quality	**C** patterns	**D** levels

20 Staff negotiations

Vocabulary

1 Complete these negotiating dialogues by writing a word or phrase from the box in each space.

accept	acceptable	come back	consult	however	possibility	prepared
question	saying	~~suggest~~	thing	think		

A Here's what we **1** .suggest.: €2,000 upfront and the balance on delivery.

B No, I'm afraid we couldn't possibly **2** ...... that. What we want is €1,000 upfront and the balance at 30 days.

A For us, the most important **3** ...... is a commitment to delivery times and a penalty clause if they are missed.

B I'll have to **4** ...... about that, but it might be all right.

A What we'd like first of all is a reduction in the number of staff on temporary contracts.

B I'm afraid that's out of the **5** .... It would reduce our flexibility.

A Well, here's another **6** .... How about if we agree to more flexible working in return for a reduction in temporary contracts?

B We'd have to **7** ...... on that one. Can we **8** ...... to you on that later?

A We'd like 5% now and another 5% next year.

B So, what you're **9** ...... is basically 10% spread over two years and then pay increases in line with inflation for the following two years?

A That's right.

B I guess the pay increases in line with inflation are **10** ......, but we're not **11** ...... to accept the 5% plus 5%. **12** ...... , we could offer 6% this year and then pay increases in line with inflation after that.

2 Complete the expressions in these sentences by writing one word in each space.

1 We've been working round the .... to complete the order on time.

2 When I asked him to attend a training course, he got very hot under the .... and told me he should be leading the training course, not attending it!

3 I think management should put their money where their .... is and offer us an incentive package.

4 Stan is feeling pretty frustrated with his job because he's been .... over for promotion yet again.

5 Monica's work wasn't up to .... , so we had to terminate her contract.

6 I'd like a bit more responsibility and not have my boss breathing down my .... all day at the office.

Grammar

1 Match these sentence halves to make conditional sentences.

1 As long as their rents stay low,
2 Had our company done proper financial planning,
3 If it weren't for the interest rates,
4 If we were to carry out another sales forecast now,
5 Because of the disappointing sales campaign,
6 Providing our workforce accept a low salary increase,

a it wouldn't have gone bankrupt last March.
b we'll have to increase our marketing effort next year.
c we'll be able to cover costs.
d we'd be making a tidy profit now.
e we'd be able to set more realistic production targets.
f they should be able to stay in the same offices.

2 Write sentences which are true about you, starting with the words given.

1 Had my company ... / Had I ...
2 As long as I work ...
3 If it weren't for my ...
4 In the event of my ...
5 Providing I don't ...
6 If my boss were to ...

Reading

Write one word in each space in this memo, which Sylvie Ballarin wrote after the staff–management negotiations on page 97 of your Student's Book.

Memo

To: Board of directors
From: Human resources director
Subject: Negotiations on relocation of staff

A meeting was **1** .held.. on May 21st between staff representatives and the management negotiating team **2** .... the objective of finalising an agreement on relocation in line with management plans. The **3** .... points were agreed on:

• We accepted our staff representatives' request that all 90 employees should have the option of relocating, **4** .... the basis that it is unlikely that this **5** .... occur. Our own calculations show that somewhere in the region of 30 staff will accept voluntary redundancy **6** .... than relocate.
• We agreed to a 6% increase **7** .... salary but were unwilling to accept staff representatives' demand for an across-the-board promotion of all staff. **8** .... was agreed that this would be based strictly **9** .... merit.
• We agreed to a £15,000 one-off payment to cover the cost of the move irrespective of the number of family members involved **10** .... the changes. This would avoid discriminating against people with smaller families, **11** .... were more likely to wish to move in any **12** ....
• We furthermore accepted that no one would be **13** .... redundant against their **14** .... and that voluntary redundancies would be encouraged with a payment of two months' gross salary over and **15** .... employees' legal entitlement.

Sylvie Ballarin
Human resources director

21 Corporate ethics

Vocabulary

Rewrite these sentences using the words given in brackets.

1 He didn't meet his targets, but fortunately he warned us that he wouldn't. (*least*)
  He didn't meet his targets, but at least he warned us that
  he wouldn't.

2 To express the idea in an uncomplicated way, the capitalist system is the most efficient economic system devised to date. (*simply put*)

3 All I want to say is that it was a badly thought-out project. (*merely*)

4 When you take everything into account, his work was a surprising success. (*considered*)

5 I expected her to be sending me the contract last week. (*supposedly*)
  She was …

6 We thought we had an exclusive agreement with these suppliers, but we discovered that they were supplying our competitors at the same time as well. (*all the while*)

7 We were advised that they were in breach of contract and for this reason we had the contract terminated. (*thus*)

8 He may be totally incompetent, but one good thing is that he is honest. (*least*)

Grammar

Complete these sentences by writing the correct article (*a*, *an* or *the*) or leaving the space blank (–) if no article is required.

1 I've left ...a.... letter and .... fax in your in-tray. You can leave .... fax till after .... weekend, but I think you should deal with .... letter today.

2 That was quite .... useful piece of .... advice you gave me yesterday.

3 I'm phoning you because we're hoping to change .... office furniture. We want to give .... office .... more up-to-date look.

4 I'll be back in .... hour. I'm just going out to have .... bite of .... lunch.

5 We're looking for .... investors to put .... money into .... business, otherwise our expansion plans will come to nothing.

6 .... business world is .... tough place. Don't go into .... business unless you're prepared for .... hard work.

7 When do you think .... company will start to make .... profit? This is .... most worrying time of my life.

8 Do you think .... Spanish would be interested in our products?

9 When we first put .... product on .... market, it didn't sell at all well. However, when .... economy picked up, ... sales picked up as well and now it's .... great success.

10 .... changing jobs is .... inevitable part of .... business life. No one nowadays can expect to stay in .... same job for ever.

Reading

Choose the best option, A, B, C or D, to complete this article.

The Day Chocolate Company

Our mission at the Day Chocolate Company is to improve the **1** .. livelihood. of small-scale cocoa farmers in West Africa. Our business is to **2** .... *Divine* fair-trade chocolate in the UK market, one of the most competitive and valuable markets in the world. To do this, we have had to **3** .... some of the most hard-nosed people in the UK retail **4** .... As the products are good and the profit **5** .... reasonable, they have been **6** .... to give us shelf space.

There is a **7** .... appetite among UK consumers for fair-trade products, products that deliver real benefit for producers in developing countries, products that **8** .... them feel they can really make a difference.

This increased demand has **9** .... to more interest from retailers, who have **10** .... an increasing range of products, and even developed **11** ....-label fair-trade ranges. Ultimately, there has even been interest from multinational corporations like Nestlé. They are all **12** .... to a growing consumer demand, and while increasing numbers of people in Britain are looking for products and services from companies that are powered by their principles, the **13** .... for social enterprise is good.

But the challenges are still the same; **14** .... finance to fund our growth is still difficult. In the main, we are companies without assets to **15** .... loans.

from *The Observer*

1	A	lifeline	B	lifetime	C	livelihood	D	lifespan
2	A	establish	B	found	C	set	D	place
3	A	come round	B	win over	C	talk into	D	bring out
4	A	division	B	section	C	segment	D	sector
5	A	values	B	benefits	C	margins	D	slices
6	A	prepared	B	agreed	C	accepted	D	compliant
7	A	rising	B	growing	C	widening	D	deepening
8	A	make	B	have	C	get	D	do
9	A	caused	B	resulted	C	risen	D	led
10	A	stored	B	stacked	C	stashed	D	stocked
11	A	white	B	own	C	their	D	blank
12	A	answering	B	changing	C	reciprocating	D	responding
13	A	forecast	B	outlook	C	expectancy	D	prevision
14	A	lifting	B	rising	C	rousing	D	raising
15	A	ensure	B	assure	C	secure	D	insure

(1 C livelihood is circled)

22 Expanding abroad

Vocabulary

1 Match these adjectives describing personal qualities (1–8) with their definitions (a–h). Can you remember which ones were used about Charles Banks in Unit 22 of the Student's Book?

1 big-headed
2 far-sighted

3 hard-driving
4 hard-headed

5 straight-talking
6 tight-fisted

7 tight-lipped
8 two-faced

a working hard and forcing others to work hard too
b having good judgement about what will be needed in the future and making wise decisions based on this
c honest and direct
d not influenced by emotions
e not sincere, saying unpleasant things about people while seeming to be pleasant when they are with you
f thinking that you are more important or more clever than you really are
g unwilling to speak about something
h unwilling to spend money

2 Complete these sentences with the adjectives describing personal qualities from Exercise 1.

1 He turned out to be really far-sighted. when he invested in IBM all those years ago, before computers had even been invented.
2 If he was my assistant, I'd have fired him ages ago. He's so .... ! He smiles and is charming to his boss's face, then criticises her behind her back.
3 In their .... approach to business, they see long-term growth as more important than short-term shareholder profit.
4 Our company finance director is extremely .... , so don't expect any budget increase from him.
5 People in the company regularly work 12-hour days under the influence of our .... boss.
6 She's become really .... since she was promoted and seems to think that she's the only one who can do the job.
7 She's pretty .... and will leave you in no doubt if she thinks your performance is not up to scratch.
8 They left the meeting .... , so we got no indication of how the negotiations had fared.

3 Complete these sentences using the words from the box.

1 After a period of ..sustained. growth, our sales have started to level off.

2 I can't imagine him applying for another job – his .... to this company is so strong that I don't think he'll ever want to retire.

3 In order to win investment, you'll have to demonstrate evidence of a .... business approach.

4 Jan Pollock is a .... member of our financial management team.

5 One of the things that keeps us ahead of our rivals is our single-minded .... of excellence.

<table>
<tr><td>commitment</td></tr>
<tr><td>complacent</td></tr>
<tr><td>diverse</td></tr>
<tr><td>driver</td></tr>
<tr><td>key</td></tr>
<tr><td>leverage</td></tr>
<tr><td>pursuit</td></tr>
<tr><td>sound</td></tr>
<tr><td>sustained</td></tr>
<tr><td>synergies</td></tr>
</table>

6 Our organisation is made up of a variety of very different businesses, and by moving people across businesses, we create .... which make the organisation extremely dynamic.

7 The company is active in fields as .... as cosmetics, software and tourism.

8 The need to keep ahead of the competition is the main .... in our strategy of continuous innovation.

9 They went bankrupt because they became .... and didn't keep abreast of new developments in the market.

10 We have used our international reputation for excellence to .... us into a position as market leaders in our field.

4 Match the beginnings of these sentences (1–9) with the most suitable endings (a–i).

1 After the disaster, the insurance companies paid out
2 I don't think they're going to pay up

3 I'll call in at the bank on my way home and pay in
4 She just popped into
5 That strategy won't pay off

6 They took advantage of
7 We aim to pay off

8 We're buying the company in order to break into
9 When they took over

a his office to answer his query.
b millions in compensation to the victims.

c the cheques.

d the loan in less than five years.
e the low share price to take control of the firm.
f the Scandinavian market.
g their main Taiwanese rival, what they really benefited from was economies of scale.
h unless they allocate it enough in the budget.
i unless we put a lawyer onto them.

5 Complete these sentences in any way you like.

1 I go to the bank every morning to pay in ...
2 It'll take more than ten years to pay off ...
3 The last time I popped into ...
4 When clients don't pay up, ...
5 You should take advantage of ...

An overseas partnership

Grammar

1 Join these sentences using the word(s) in brackets.

1 You'll finish the report. Send it to me immediately. (*as soon as*)
   As soon as you've finished the report, send it to me.

2 You'll be writing the report. Include statistics. (*when*)

3 You're going to speak to all the sales staff. They are coming to Head Office next week. (*when*)

4 He will be promoted to manager next week. He won't be so friendly. (*after*)

5 The offices are going to be redecorated. Meanwhile, we shall take our annual holidays. (*while*)

6 You'll have to be careful not to exceed your expense account. You'll be visiting Berlin next month. (*when*)

7 You're going to write to them. Visit their website first. (*before*)

8 He'll go home. We'll change the details. (*after*)

2 Write complex sentences using all the information below. You can make any changes necessary to the words given.

1 our company – world leader – manufacturer of floor tiles – made of marble – based near Cremona (Italy)
   Our company, which is a world leader in the manufacture
   of marble floor tiles, is based near Cremona, Italy.

2 tiles – exported to many parts of Europe + Middle East – marble – produced locally – top quality

3 investigating possibility: opening offices in your country ➝ market products – your region

4 contacting you because looking for local distributor/collaborator with chain of outlets + interested stocking our products

5 Luigi Bossano – marketing director – will visit area – near future – meet potential distributors

6 interested? – tell us when his visit convenient

7 enclose brochure + company literature ➝ clearer idea – products + company

3 Rewrite these sentences using the words or phrases given in brackets.

1 The production line was halted due to an electrical fault. (*because there*)
   The production line was halted because there was an electrical fault.

2 I missed the meeting because the dates got mixed up. (*owing to*)

3 She was able to sort out the problem because Mr Bossano helped her. (*thanks to*)

4 I'll visit you with samples of our new products at any time which is suitable to you. (*whenever it*)

5 On arrival, you should come directly to my office. (*when you*)
6 I've visited the new offices they are building on the outskirts of the city. (*being*)
7 Any money which you spend on advertising is wasted. (*spent*)
8 Please visit Mr Lee during your visit to Singapore. (*while*)
9 She behaved rudely, and that's why the meeting was a failure. (*due to*)
10 We won't be going ahead with the project because it costs too much. (*on account of*)

Reading

In most lines of this letter there is one wrong word. Cross out the wrong word and write the correct word on the right. If the line is correct, put a tick (✓).

Dear Mr Zhao		
Thank you for your letter of March 14th in ~~where~~ you	1	which
mention the possibility of visiting our country with the	2	
intention of opening out a market for your services. I	3	
apologise for not replying earlier; that was due to the fact	4	
that I myself was on an overseas travel until just this week.	5	
We would indeed be interested in meeting you. Like you	6	
probably know, we are a specialist provider of financial	7	
advices for small private investors in high-technology firms	8	
based on Western Europe. Many of our clients would	9	
welcome the possibility of extending their portfolios for	10	
include similar firms located in the Far East (your area of	11	
specialisation). Similar, as you state in your letter, since	12	
many of your clients has expressed an interest in the	13	
European market, I believe we would be well placed to	14	
provide the sort of informations they require.	15	
A collaboration between our two firms could be particularly	16	
fruitfully for both, and I would welcome the opportunity to	17	
discuss this with yourself.	18	
I am available for since a meeting whenever it is convenient	19	
for you. Please contact me by email to arrange this. We	20	
would too be delighted to arrange your hotel	21	
accommodation and any another details of your trip.	22	
For your interest, I enclosed a variety of company literature	23	
of the type we send to our clients.	24	
I very much look forward to hear from you.	25	
Frank Legrange		

UNIT 24 A planning conference

Vocabulary

1 Find words or phrases in the extracts on pages 114 and 115 of the Student's Book which mean the following.

1 more complicated (extract A) +rickier
2 get rid of by exchanging it for something else (extract A)
3 too shocking or unlikely to be imagined as possible (extract B)
4 serious accidents or disasters (extract B)
5 stealing from the company (extract B)
6 unexpected and inconvenient or unpleasant (extract B)
7 understand something, especially something difficult (extract C)
8 making more modern by adding new information (extract C)
9 cause confusion and disorder (extract C)
10 very bad (extract C)
11 deceived, tricked (extract C)
12 was subjected to careful and detailed examination (extract D)
13 suddenly and unexpectedly, from one day to the next (extract D)
14 damaging and destructive (extract D)
15 had legal action taken against it (extract E)
16 were given bad reports in the media (extract E)
17 acts that are criminal or bad (extract E)
18 spoil the reputation of (extract E)

2 Choose the best option, A, B, C or D, to complete these sentences.

1 The difficulty of managing risk is that managers have to examine a range of possible outcomes .
   A outlets   B outputs   C outcomes   D outgoings
2 Risk is trickier to   than many other challenges.
   A handle   B deal   C work   D cope
3 Several of the decisions he took   to be wrong.
   A came out   B brought out   C worked out   D turned out
4 Global supply chains   companies to risks which would have been unthinkable a century ago.
   A uncover   B disclose   C expose   D reveal
5 You should monitor and track your risks as you   .
   A go about   B go along   C go by   D pass by
6 Companies set up complicated security systems to   penetration by computer hackers.
   A escape from   B hold against   C guard against   D hold up
7 The Internet has   improved the transparency of company activities.
   A very   B extremely   C totally   D greatly
8 It is becoming increasingly difficult for companies to   secrets.
   A hold   B keep   C grasp   D cover

9 Managers will inevitably be ...... responsible for their staff's misdeeds.
   A held   **B** taken   **C** accounted   **D** said

10 When the company ...... scrutiny by the police, its clients left overnight.
   A came in for   **B** came in to   **C** fell into   **D** came under

3 Complete these sentences with the correct prepositions.

1 The brand never took ..off.. , despite heavy investments in advertising.

2 Risk management does not lend itself .... forecasts or plans.

3 If you are not prepared .... risk, you should not be in business.

4 Risks can range .... earthquakes .... stealing by senior managers.

5 Some risks are easier to deal .... than others.

6 Our organisation has spent millions .... updating the computer system and invested heavily .... new software.

7 We decided to pull .... of the Japanese market after losing a lot of money there.

8 I'm concerned .... the problems which might arise if we are given a bad press.

Grammar

Change these sentences, starting with the words given.

1 Although he spent a lot of time on risk management, he didn't manage to identify the risk which would eventually ruin the company.
Despite ...*spending a lot of time on risk management, he didn't manage to identify the risk which would eventually ruin the company*...

2 Although it may seem surprising, companies' reputations may be damaged by their competitors' misdeeds.
Surprising as ...

3 Despite their heavy exposure to risk, the company continues to invest in new technology shares.
Even though ...

4 However risk-averse you are, it is absolutely essential to make this investment.
Even if you ...

5 We will abide by any decision you make.
Whatever decision ...

6 We will make sure of a successful outcome to the project, even if it takes a very long time.
However long ...

7 Difficult though the investigation has been, I think we have at last got to the truth.
In spite of ...

8 Despite working here for 30 years, he never progressed beyond a clerical role.
Although ...

Word list

Some of these words appear in the transcripts at the end of the Student's Book.
U= unit, T = track, so *U1 T1* means Unit 1 Track 1.

A

absenteeism *n* (p 85) employees not being at work when they should be

account for *v* (p 51) form the total of something

acquisition *n* (p 104) buying new companies

across the board *adv* (U17 T6) happening or having an effect on people at every level and in every area

administer *v* (p 17) manage or govern

adversarial *adj* (p 83) involving opposition or disagreement

advertising campaign *n* (p 46) organised programme of advertisements, usually concerning promoting a certain product or brand

advocate *n* (p 101) person who supports an idea (or product)

agenda *n* (p 22) list of matters to be discussed at a meeting

alignment *n* (U22 T14) agreement between people who want to work together because of shared interests or aims

allocate *v* (p 33) give something to someone as their share of a total amount, for them to use in a particular way

allot *v* (p 23) give (especially a share of something available) for a particular purpose

angel *n* (p 69) wealthy person who invests money in new business projects

appraise *v* (p 57) examine someone or something in order to judge their qualities, success or needs

approach *n* (p 83) way of considering something

assembly *n* (p 83) process of putting together the parts of a machine or structure

assembly line *n* (p 83) line of machines and workers in a factory which a product moves along while it is being built or produced. Each machine or worker performs a particular job, which must be completed before the product moves to the next position in the line

assess *v* (p 17) judge or decide the amount, value, quality or importance of something

asset *n* (p 31) something valuable belonging to a person or organisation which can be used for the payment of debts

attendee *n* (p 24) someone who goes to a place, event, etc.

autocratic *adj* (p 10) demanding absolute obedience from other people

axe *n* (p 66) way to reduce the number of employees

B

backer *n* (p 69) person who gives financial support to something

backup plan *n* (p 65) scheme ready to be used in place of or to help another

balance sheet *n* (p 67) statement that shows the value of a company's assets and its debts

bang heads together *v* (U13 T22) when two or more people get together to work out complicated issues, usually involving some argument, before reaching a solution

bank charge *n* (p 72) sum of money paid by a customer for a bank's services

bankable *adj* (U14 T23) likely to make money

banner ad *n* (p 46) form of advertising on the World Wide Web which involves putting a wide and short, or tall and narrow advert on an interesting web page

barcode *n* (p 48) small rectangular pattern of thick and thin black lines of magnetic ink printed on an item, or on its container, so that its details can be read by and recorded on a computer system

bargaining point *n* (p 77) something which someone else wants that you are willing to lose in order to reach an agreement

be in a position to *v* (p 74) be able to do something, usually because you have the necessary experience, authority or money

benchmark *v* (p 33) measure the quality of something by comparing it with something else of an accepted standard

benefits *pl n* (p 101) things such as medical insurance that employees receive in addition to money

better off *adj* (p 101) richer

bid for *v* (p 34) offer to do some work for a particular price

bid *v* (p 32) compete against other firms by offering to do a job or

contract for a certain amount of money

blue-collar worker *n* (p 86) worker who does unskilled work rather than office work

board *n* (p 12) group of people who are responsible for controlling and organising a company or organisation

bonus *n* (p 10) extra amount of money that is given to you as a present or reward in addition to the money you were expecting

bookkeeping *n* (p 72) job of keeping a record of the money that has been spent or received by a business

bottom line *n* (p 12) final line in the accounts of a company or organisation, which states the total profit or loss that has been made

brand awareness *n* (p 46) knowledge of a particular make of product

brand builder *n* (p 15) developer of a product's image

brand identity *n* (p 32) see *brand image*

brand image *n* (p 15) impression of a product in the minds of potential customers

brand management *n* (p 17) how a company manages its brands and brand image

breadwinner *n* (U20 T11) member of a family who earns the money that the family needs

break even *v* (p 102) make neither a loss nor a profit doing business

briefing *n* (p 106) meeting where information and instructions are given

brochure *n* (p 51) type of small magazine that contains pictures and information on a product or a company

budget *n* (p 18) plan to show how much money an organisation will earn and how much they will need or be able to spend

buoyant *adj* (p 91) healthy and strong

buzz session *n* (U16 T4) activity where a group of people make lots of suggestions quickly

by the book *adv* (p 10) formally, or according to the rules

C

calibre *n* (U22 T14) degree of quality or excellence of someone

call-centre operative *n* (p 29) person who works in an office where large numbers of telephone calls, especially from customers, are handled for an organisation

camaraderie *n* (p 82) feeling of friendliness towards people with whom you work or share an experience

capitalise on *v* (p 42) use to your advantage

career break *n* (p 89) period in which a person decides to leave their job temporarily

career continuity *n* (U18 T7) ability to continue your professional career

cash cow *n* (U14 T23) very profitable business or part of the business

cash *n* (p 72) money which is immediately available

churn out *v* (U19 T9) produce large amounts of something quickly, usually of low quality

cipher *n* (p 83) a person or group of people without power, but used by others for their own purposes, or someone who is not important

classified ad/advertisement *n* (p 46) small advertisement placed in a

newspaper by a person wishing to buy or sell something, offer or get employment, etc.

close down *v* (U20 T11) if a business or organisation closes down, or someone closes it down, it stops operating

clutch *n* (p 106) handful

cold-calling *n* (p 58) when a person in business telephones or visits a possible customer to try to sell them something without being asked by the customer to do so

collate *v* (U13 T22) bring together different pieces of written information

come under scrutiny *v* (p 115) subject to careful and thorough examination

competency *n* (p 65) important skill that is needed to do a job

competitive *adj* (p 82) competitive prices, services, etc. are as good as, or better than, other prices, services, etc.

compliance *n* (p 103) when people obey an order, rule or request

compromise *n* (p 77) agreement in an argument in which the people involved reduce their demands or change their opinion in order to agree

concierge service *n* (p 60) doorkeeper or porter services

consolidate *v* (p 42) combine several things, especially businesses, so that they become more effective

constraint *n* (p 73) something which controls what you do by keeping you within particular limits

contingency plan *n* (p 114) programme of action designed for handling possible future circumstances or events

corporate catering service *n* (p 54) business of providing food service to businesses (usually at a remote site)

corporate social responsibility (CSR) *n* (p 100) proposal that organisations should be obliged to make decisions based not only on financial/economic factors but also on the social and environmental consequences of their activities

count on *v* (U13 T22) be confident that you can depend on (something/someone)

credit limit *n* (p 72) maximum amount of money a bank will allow you to borrow

credit worthiness *n* (p 72) calculation of someone's ability to pay back money which they have borrowed

creditor *n* (p 67) someone to whom money is owed

crisis management *n* (p 17) process of dealing with difficult situations

critical path *n* (p 33) sequence of stages determining the minimum time needed for the execution of an entire project

crop *n* (U21 T13) (total amount gathered of) a plant such as a grain, fruit or vegetable grown in large amounts

cross-selling *n* (p 31) suggestion that customers buy additional or related accessories or products during or just after their primary purchase

current asset *n* (p 67) something owned by a business that it does not expect to keep for more than 12 months

customer base *n* (p 106) regular customers

customer care *n* (p 29) protection and service provided to customers

customer loyalty *n* (p 46) when a customer favours a certain brand or company over others (the company sometimes offers financial or other rewards for this favouritism)

customise *v* (p 50) make or change something according to the buyer's or user's needs

cut back *v* (U20 T12) use in smaller amounts

cut of the profits *n* (U18 T8) share in the profits

D

deadline *n* (p 36) time or day by which something must be done

deadlock *n* (p 77) situation in which agreement in an argument cannot be reached because neither side will change its demands or accept the demands of the other side

dealings *pl n* (p 23) activities involving other people, especially in business

debtor *n* (p 67) someone who owes money

decline *v* (p 55) gradually become less, worse, or lower

deficit *n* (p 70) amount of money a company has lost during a particular period of time

delegate *v* (p 14) give a particular job, duty, right, etc. to someone else so that they do it for you

deposit *n* (U16 T5) sum of money which is given in advance as part of a total payment for something

depreciation *n* (p 67) loss of value of an asset such as machinery over time

direct response advertising *n* (U10 T18) form of advertising designed to obtain a direct response between the viewer and the advertiser: the customer responds to the marketer directly

discharge a debt *v* (p 100) pay a debt completely

disclose v (p 57) make something known publicly, or show something that was secret

disposable income n (p 43) money which you can spend as you want and not the money which you spend on taxes, food and other basic needs

distribution n (p 43) making goods available to customers

diverse footprint n (p 105) varied area over which something is present

dividend n (p 67) (a part of) the profit of a company that is paid to the people who own shares in it

dotcom n (p 11) Internet company

double-digit adj (p 104) number with two digits (i.e. between 10 and 99 inclusive)

downside n (U19 T9) disadvantage of a situation

downsize v (p 87) if you downsize a company or organisation, you make it smaller by reducing the number of people working for it, and if it downsizes, it becomes smaller in this way

draw up v (p 79) prepare something, usually something official, in writing

dress code n (p 10) set of rules for what you can wear

dwindle v (p 55) become smaller in size or amount, or fewer in number

E

economic downturn n (p 102) reduction in a country's financial activity

economies of scale pl n (p 110) where the costs of production fall as a business grows in size

emerging market n (p 67) area or country where there is growing demand for goods

empire n (p 15) very large and important business organisation

enhance v (U5 T11) improve the quality, amount or strength of something

entrant n (U6 T13) person who takes part in a competition or an examination

envision v (p 77) form a mental picture of something, typically something that may occur or be possible in the future

e-sale n (p 52) sales transaction performed digitally, usually over the Internet

estimate v (p 34) guess the cost, size, value, etc. of something

ethics pl n (p 100) a system of accepted beliefs which control behaviour, especially such a system based on morals

evict v (U16 T5) force someone to leave somewhere

excess production capacity n (p 92) ability of a factory to produce more than it actually does

executive summary n (U14 T24) overview of the main points of a business plan or proposal

expertise n (p 105) high level of knowledge or skill

exposure n (p 48) experience of something

extend your overdraft v (U15 T2) lengthen the period of time before you have to pay back the money you have overdrawn

F

factor n (p 41) fact or situation which influences the result of something

factoring n (p 72) system of buying debts for less than they are worth and then obtaining payment for them from the debtors

fall short *v* (p 65) fail to reach a target

faulty *adj* (p 100) not perfectly made or not working correctly

feasibility *n* (p 70) whether something can be done, made or achieved

fee *n* (U6 T13) amount of money paid for a particular piece of work

feedback *n* (p 15) remarks passed back to the person responsible, so that changes can be made if necessary

field *n* (p 82) area of activity or interest

fire *v* (p 15) dismiss

fixed asset *n* (p 67) building, equipment or land owned by a company

flexible working *n* (p 88) working without strict times for starting and finishing

flutter *n* (p 69) small bet

foreign exchange fluctuation *n* (p 42) rises and falls in the currencies of other countries

freelancer *n* (p 86) worker who does particular pieces of work for different organisations, rather than working all the time for a single organisation

frontline staff *n* (p 29) employees with direct contact with customers

FTSE 100 *n* (p 106) *Financial Times* Stock Exchange 100 index; the main measure of the amount by which the leading 100 shares sold on the London Stock Exchange have gone up or down in value

G

gadget *n* (U19 T9) small device or machine with a particular purpose

gain ground (on) *v* (p 42) make progress at the expense of

get a bad press *v* (p 115) receive criticism from the media

get down to business *v* (p 79) start talking about the subject to be discussed

get down to work *v* (p 14) start to direct your efforts and attention towards work

get off the ground *v* (U23 T17) if a plan or activity gets off the ground or you get it off the ground, it starts or succeeds

get on board *v* (p 60) make (someone) part of a group or team, or become part of a group or team

get (something) straight *v* (p 79) understand correctly, or make something clear

get your desk clear *v* (U20 T10) finish all your work

glitch *n* (p 92) small problem or fault that prevents something from working well

global presence *n* (U23 T17) if a company has a global presence, it sells its products all over the world

go bankrupt *v* (p 56) become unable to pay what you owe, and have control of your financial matters given, by a court of law, to a person who sells your property to pay your debts

go bust *v* (p 65) if a company goes bust, it is forced to close because it is financially unsuccessful

go on a hunch *v* (U13 T22) act on an idea which is based on feeling and for which there is no proof

go out of business *v* (U6 T13) no longer able to operate as a business

goal *n* (p 10) aim or purpose

going rate *n* (U18 T8) standard rate of payment for a particular job

goodwill *n* (p 67) value of the popularity, the regular customers, etc. of a business calculated as part of its worth when being sold

gross profit *n* (p 24) company's profit before certain costs and taxes are deducted

ground-breaking *adj* (p 111) if something is ground-breaking, it is very new and a big change from other things of its type

H

halve *v* (p 55) if something halves, it is reduced by half

hands-on approach *n* (p 14) way of doing things which is practical, not theoretical

have a bearing on sth *v* (U13 T22) have an influence on something or a relationship to something

have your hands in the till *v* (p 114) steal money from the place where you work

high-profile *adj* (p 70) attracting a lot of attention and interest from the public and newspapers, television, etc.

hire *v* (p 69) employ someone or pay them to do a particular job

hire and fire *v* (p 92) employ and dismiss

home working *n* (p 88) working at home, while communicating with your office by telephone, fax or computer

horse-trading *n* (p 77) negotiation which requires bargaining and each side reducing their demands

hunch *n* (U13 T22) see *go on a hunch*

I

impact *n* (p 83) powerful effect that something, especially something new, has on a situation or person

in line with *adv* (p 78) at the same level as

in place *adv* (p 114) organised

in sync *adj* (p 66) at the same time or the same speed

in the pipeline *adv* (p 109) being planned and developed

incentive *n* (p 24) something which encourages a person to do something

incentive payment *n* (p 94) financial reward to stimulate action from staff or customers

incompetent *adj* (p 15) showing lack of ability or skill to do something successfully

in-house magazine *n* (p 18) publication which is written and produced within an organisation by its employees

input *n* (p 20) something, such as advice, information or effort, that is provided in order to help something succeed or develop

insight *n* (p 65) (the ability to have) a clear, deep and sometimes sudden understanding of a complicated problem or situation

internal candidate *n* (p 25) person seeking a position who already holds another job within the organisation

interview panel *n* (p 25) group of people who ask candidates questions to see if they are suitable for a job

issue *n* (p 22) subject or problem which people are thinking and talking about

item *n* (p 19) one of several subjects to be considered

itemise *v* (p 32) list things separately

J

job sharing *n* (p 88) doing part of a job with someone else, so that each person works part-time

joint-venture partner *n* (p 43) associate in a commercial enterprise which is undertaken jointly

jot down v (p 79) write something quickly on a piece of paper so that you remember it

K

key adj (p 67) very important and having a lot of influence on other people or things

key stage n (p 33) important time period in a sequence of events

knock-on effect n (p 101) when an event or situation has a knock-on effect, it indirectly causes other events or situations

knock (something) off the price v (U16 T4) give a discount off the price

knowledge worker n (p 86) person whose work requires specialist knowledge

L

labour intensive adj (p 91) needing a lot of workers

landlord n (p 79) person or organisation that owns a building or an area of land and is paid by other people for the use of it

lay off v (p 82) stop employing (someone), sometimes temporarily, because there is no money to pay them or because there is no work for them

layoff n (p 66) when someone stops employing someone, sometimes temporarily, because there is no money to pay them or because there is no work for them

lead time n (p 92) time needed to design and develop a new product

leafleting n (U22 T14) giving out leaflets to people

lease n (p 76) legal agreement in which you pay money in order to use a building, piece of land, vehicle, etc. for a period

leaseholder n (p 78) person who pays the owner of a piece of land, a building, etc. in order to be able to use it

legal entitlement n (U20 T12) something that, in law, you have the right to do or have, or when you have the right to do or have something

leverage n (p 77) power to influence people and get the results you want

liability n (p 60) when you are legally responsible for something

liability n (p 67) debt

life insurance n (p 54) system in which you make regular payments to an insurance company in exchange for a fixed amount of money which will be paid to someone you have named, usually a member of your family, when you die

limited liability company n (U24 T19) if this type of business goes bankrupt, then the owners will only risk the money they have invested in the company

line management n (p 17) direct management of staff

line of business n (p 105) particular kind of commercial enterprise

loan n (p 69) sum of money which is borrowed, often from a bank, and has to be paid back, usually together with an additional amount of money that you have to pay as a charge for borrowing

logo n (p 70) design or symbol used by a company to advertise its products

loss adjuster n (U18 T8) person who works for an insurance company and decides how much money should be paid out in each case of something having been damaged or lost

lucrative *adj* (U13 T22) producing a lot of money, profitable

lump sum *n* (U16 T5) sum of money that is paid in one large amount on one occasion

M

machine tool *n* (p 54) mechanically operated tool for cutting or shaping wood, metals, etc.

mainstream *adj* (U13 T22) desired by most people

make redundant *v* (p 12) no longer employ someone because there is not enough work

management reporting *n* (U22 T14) monthly report(s) on financial performance produced by management for shareholders

mandatory *adj* (p 103) describes something which must be done, or which is demanded by law

manufacturing base *n* (U19 T9) all the companies producing goods in a country or region

map *v* (p 33) make a plan in detail

margin *n* (U11 T19) amount by which revenue from sales exceeds cost of sales

market share *n* (p 12) percentage of all the sales within a market that are held by one brand or company

marketing-led *adj* (U24 T18) influenced by customers' needs (as opposed to being product-led)

memo *n* (p 18) message or other information in writing sent by one person or department to another in the same business organisation

mentor *n* (p 10) person who gives another person help and advice over a period of time and often also teaches them how to do their job

middle management *n* (p 17) level between senior management and junior management

mid-size *adj* (p 60) describes something that is neither large nor small

miscellaneous *adj* (p 70) consisting of a mixture of various things which are not usually connected with each other

monitor *v* (p 12) watch and check a situation carefully for a period of time in order to discover something about it

morale *n* (p 65) amount of confidence felt by a person or group of people, especially when in a dangerous or difficult situation

N

natural wastage *n* (p 91) reduction in the number of people who work for an organisation which is achieved by not replacing those people who leave

network *v* (p 57) meet people who might be useful to know, especially in your job

niche market *n* (p 42) small area of trade within the economy, often involving specialised products

nose-dive, take a *v* (U13 T22) fall or drop suddenly and by a great deal

O

offset *v* (p 70) balance one influence against an opposing influence, so that there is no great difference as a result

on site *adv* (p 59) inside a factory, office building, etc.

one-off payment *n* (U20 T12) money that is paid only once

one-to-one interview *n* (p 18) meeting between just two people

ongoing *adj* (U22 T14) continuing to exist or develop, or happening at the present moment

operating profit *n* (p 67) measure of profit that a business earns on its normal operations

order book *n* (p 73) book in which a company or shop keeps a record of customers' orders

out of pocket *adj* (U20 T12) having less money than you started with

outcome *n* (p 25) result

outgoings *pl n* (p 72) amounts of money that regularly have to be spent

outlay *n* (p 37) amount of money spent for a particular purpose, especially as a first investment in something

outperform *v* (p 82) do well in a particular job or activity compared to others of a similar type

outplacement service *n* (U20 T12) professional service to help redundant employees to search for a new job, paid for by the former employer

output *n* (p 37) amount of something produced by a person, machine, factory, country, etc.

outsourcing *n* (p 29) the practice of a company paying to have part of its work done by another company

overdraft *n* (p 67) an amount of money that a customer with a bank account is temporarily allowed to owe to the bank, or the agreement which allows this

overheads *pl n* (p 37) the regular and necessary costs, such as rent and heating, that are involved in operating a business

over-the-counter sale *n* (p 52) ordinary sales transaction in a shop

overtime *n* (U18 T7) extra payment for working beyond the usual time

overtrading *n* (p 72) operating a business while not having enough money to pay creditors and employees

overview *n* (p 23) short description of something which provides general information about it, but no details

overworked *adj* (U3 T5) having to work too much

P

package *n* (U20 T11) related group of things when they are offered together as a single unit

patent *v* (p 109) register the official legal right to make or sell an invention for a particular number of years

pay off *v* (p 65) if an investment or risk pays off, it is successful

payroll *n* (p 37) list of the people employed by a company

peak *v* (p 84) reach the highest, strongest or best point, value or level of skill

peer group *n* (p 82) people who are approximately the same age as you and come from a similar social group

penalty clause *n* (p 76) part of a contract which punishes the person or organisation doing the work if it is not completed on time

penetration *n* (p 43) how much share of a particular market a company or a product manages to achieve

per capita *adv* (p 40) if you state an amount per capita, you mean that amount for each person

performance pay *n* (p 17) salary that increases when your work improves or becomes more productive

perk *n* (U17 T6) advantage or benefit given to an employee in addition to their salary, e.g. private health care or a company car

place a premium on *v* (p 87) especially value

player *n* (U8 T15) important company involved in a market or industry

plummet *v* (p 55) fall very quickly and suddenly

point on the pay scale *n* (U20 T10) position on the salary scale which shows different rates of pay depending on your job and your seniority

point-of-sale display *n* (p 46) visual presentation for promotional purposes at the place where goods are sold

pop-up box (also **pop-up ad/pop-up**) *n* (U10 T17) form of online advertising on the World Wide Web when certain websites open a new window to display advertisements

premise *n* (p 101) idea or theory on which a statement or action is based

premises *pl n* (p 67) land and buildings owned by someone, especially by a company or organisation

presence *n* (U23 T17) see *global presence*

pre-tax profit *n* (p 67) money which is earned in trade or business before taxes have been paid

procedure *n* (p 23) set of actions which is the official or accepted way of doing something

proceedings *pl n* (p 23) series of events that happen in a planned and controlled way

procurement *n* (U6 T12) the obtaining of supplies

production capacity *n* (p 42) total amount of resources available to achieve maximum output

productive *adj* (p 25) useful

product-led *adj* (p 92) activities are determined by the requirements of the product (as opposed to customer-led or marketing-led)

profit and loss account *n* (p 67) financial statement that summarises the expenses, losses and overheads of a company, used to calculate the net profit

profit margin *n* (p 31) profit that can be made in a business or sale after costs have been subtracted

profitability *n* (p 31) capacity to make a profit

progressive *adj* (p 101) encouraging change in the way that things are done

prospect *n* (p 60) potential purchaser or customer

proven track record *n* (p 32) all the successful achievements that someone or something has had in the past

psychometric test *n* (p 25) exam to measure scientifically a person's mental capacities and personality

publicly accountable *adj* (p 11) responsible to the government

pull figures out of the air *v* (U13 T22) choose numbers in a random way, rather than one based on evidence or logic

punitive *adj* (p 73) used to describe costs which are so high they are difficult to pay, and which are often used to punish someone or limit their activities

purchase *n* (p 50) something that you buy

pursuit *n* (p 102) when you try to achieve a plan, activity, or situation, usually over a long period of time

put more on someone's plate *v* (U20 T10) give someone more work to deal with

put your money where your mouth is *v* (p 95) show that you believe in something by spending/or investing money

put up (money) *v* (p 69) provide or lend an amount of money for a particular purpose

Q

quality control *n* (p 64) process of looking at goods when they are being produced to make certain that all the goods are of the intended standard

quality management *n* (p 17) managing systems in a company so that each department works effectively and produces products or services of the required standard

quarterly *adv* (p 107) once every three months

query *n* (p 19) question

R

ranks *pl n* (p 15) the membership of a group or organisation

rate *n* (p 15) level of payment

rate *v* (p 106) judge the value or character of someone or something

rat race *n* (p 11) struggle of individuals in a competitive environment

realise *v* (U22 T14) change into money by selling

reap the benefits *v* (U14 T24) get the benefit, etc. that is the result of your own actions

recede *v* (p 55) fall

recession *n* (p 52) period when the economy of a country is not successful and conditions for business are bad

recycle *v* (p 101) collect and treat rubbish in order to produce useful materials which can be used again

red tape *n* (p 11) paperwork

referral *n* (p 60) the referring of an individual to an expert for advice

reformulate *v* (p 96) develop again all the details of a plan for doing something

registered letter *n* (U15 T2) valuable letter which, for an additional charge, can protect the sender against loss

regulation *n* (p 101) official rule

reinstall *v* (p 59) put back into position and make ready for use again

reinvest *v* (p 38) invest again

report back *v* (p 25) bring information to someone in authority

resettlement package *n* (p 96) collection of benefits offered to an employee who is relocating to another town, city or country for their work

retail outlet *n* (p 37) shop

retained earnings *pl n* (p 67) earnings which are kept by the company to invest in future projects, market research, etc.

retool *v* (p 92) change or replace machinery in a factory

retrenchment *n* (p 65) when an organisation spends less or reduces costs to avoid losing money

return *n* (p 12) amount of profit on an investment

revenue *n* (p 12) money earned from sales

reward *n* (p 83) something given in exchange for good behaviour or good work, etc.

risk management *n* (p 17) process of assessing and measuring possible dangers and evolving strategies to deal with them

risk-averse *adj* (p 61) have a strong dislike for taking risks

rocket *v* (p 52) rise extremely quickly

rota *n* (p 19) list of things that have to be done and of the people who will do them

run at a loss *v* (p 69) cost more money than is received from sales

run over time *v* (p 25) take longer than scheduled

running costs *pl n* (U14 T23) money you need to spend regularly to keep a system or organisation functioning

S

sabotage *n* (p 85) intentional damage to machines, buildings, etc.

safety procedure *n* (U20 T10) official or accepted set of actions used to keep people safe

sales force *n* (p 38) all the employees of a company whose job is persuading customers to buy their company's products or services

sales pitch *n* (U11 T19) way of talking that is intended to persuade you to buy something

sales volume *n* (U11 T19) amount of purchases made

sample *n* (p 47) group of people or things that is chosen out of a larger number and is questioned or tested in order to obtain information about the larger group

scanner *n* (p 48) device for reading information into a computer system

scenario *n* (p 65) description of possible actions or events in the future

schedule *v* (U4 T6) arrange that an event or activity will happen at a particular time

screen out *v* (p 52) filter out/remove

screening *n* (p 60) examining someone or something to discover if there is anything wrong with them/it

search engine *n* (p 53) computer program which finds information on the Internet by looking for words which you have typed in

self-employed *adj* (p 86) not working for an employer but finding work for yourself or having your own business

selling point *n* (U7 T14) characteristic of a product which will persuade people to buy it

semi-skilled *adj* (p 86) having or needing only a small amount of training

service agreement *n* (p 76) contract between two businesses where one agrees to provide a service to the other, or between a landlord and a tenant

settle your account *v* (p 74) pay all the money you owe

shareholder *n* (p 12) person who owns shares in a company

shell out *v* (U16 T5) pay, especially unwillingly

shift *n* (p 43) change in position or direction

shift *v* (U19 T9) sell

ship *v* (p 28) send goods by any form of transport to a distant place

shipper *n* (p 39) person or company whose job is to organise the sending of goods from one place to another

shop around *v* (U10 T17) compare the price and quality of the same or a

similar item in different shops
before you decide which one to buy

shop-floor worker *n* (p 85) worker in a
factory (the factory is the shop
floor)

shortage *n* (p 64) when there is not
enough of something

shortfall *n* (p 66) an amount which is
less than the level that was
expected or needed

showroom *n* (p 52) large shop in
which people are encouraged to
look at the goods that are on sale
before buying them

shrewd *adj* (U24 T18) based on a clear
understanding and good judgement
of a situation

shrink *v* (p 55) become smaller, or
make something smaller

sick leave *n* (U17 T6) absence from
work because of illness

slip *v* (p 102) go into a worse state,
often because of lack of control or
care

soar *v* (p 55) rise very quickly to a high
level

solicit *v* (p 60) ask for money,
information or help

source *v* (p 54) get something from a
particular place

specification *n* (p 32) detailed
description of how something
should be done, made, etc.

spending power *n* (p 43) ability to
purchase goods

sponsor *v* (p 69) support a person,
organisation or activity by giving
money, encouragement or other help

sponsored link *n* (p 50) text-based
advertisement which describes an
advertiser's website and the
products and services offered

spreadsheet *n* (U6 T13) computer
program, used especially in

business, which allows you to do
financial calculations and plans

staffing level *n* (U13 T22) the
numbers of employees

stake *n* (p 15) share or financial
involvement in a business

stakeholder *n* (p 101) person such as
an employee, customer or citizen
who is involved with an
organisation and therefore has an
interest in its success

stock control *n* (p 36) in a company or
shop, the system of making certain
that new supplies are ordered and
that goods have not been stolen.

stock exchange *n* (U14 T24) place
where shares in companies are
bought and sold

stock *n* (p 67) total amount of goods
available

stock price *n* (p 65) valuation of a
company's shares

stockbroker *n* (U18 T8) person or
company that buys and sells stocks
and shares for other people

stockpile *v* (p 92) build up a large store
of goods which have not been sold
yet

storage and handling facility *n* (p 42)
place or building used to store and
distribute goods

straight talking *n* (p 106) direct and
straightforward way of
communicating with others

streamline *v* (p 11) make more efficient

subcontractor *n* (p 83) person or
company that does part of a job
which another person or company
is responsible for

subsidy *n* (U21 T13) money given as
part of the cost of something, to
help or encourage it to happen

sue *v* (p 69) take legal action against a
person or organisation

summon *v* (p 23) officially arrange a meeting of people

supervision *n* (U22 T15) when someone watches a person or activity and makes certain that everything is done correctly, safely, etc.

supply base *n* (U22 T14) range of suppliers and potential suppliers

surge *v* (p 106) increase suddenly and greatly

surveillance *n* (U17 T6) the careful watching of a person or place

survey *n* (p 49) examination of opinions, behaviour, etc., made by asking people questions

sustained *adj* (p 104) continuing for a long time

symposium *n* (p 93) occasion at which people who have great knowledge of a particular subject meet in order to discuss a matter of interest

synergy *n* (p 105) the combined power of a group of things when they are working together which is greater than the total power achieved by each working separately

systems engineer *n* (p 37) person who designs and installs computer systems

T

take (someone) for a ride *v* (U10 T17) deceive or cheat (someone)

take over *v* (U22 T14) get control (of a company) by buying most of its shares

take off *v* (p 55) suddenly start to be successful or popular

target audience *n* (p 48) particular group at which advertising is aimed

target *n* (p 18) level or situation which you intend to achieve

tax exposure *n* (U7 T14) financial commitment to pay tax

tax liability *n* (p 57) amount of tax which must be paid to the government

team up with *v* (p 34) work together with

technophobe *n* (p 87) person who dislikes or fears new technology

teleworking *n* (p 88) the activity of working at home, while communicating with your office by telephone, fax or computer

temp *n* (p 86) person employed to work for a short period, especially in an office, while another person is absent or when there is extra work

tender *n* (U6 T12) formal written offer to do a job for an agreed price

time management *n* (p 17) skill of administering your time so as to work effectively

timekeeping *n* (p 18) ability to arrive at a place at the time expected

time-share holiday home *adj* (p 54) when people buy a holiday home together which each person can use for a different part of the year

track down *v* (p 60) find by searching or following tracks

trade away *v* (p 114) pass on to someone else

trade press *n* (p 33) magazine published for and read by members of a particular trade group

trade tariff *n* (U21 T13) tax collected by a government on goods coming into or sometimes going out of a country

transaction *n* (p 74) payment or business deal

transactional *adj* (p 83) in a way that is a direct business exchange

trend *n* (p 84) general development or change in a situation or in the way that people are behaving

trouble-shooting skills *pl n* (p 14) ability to remove or solve difficulties

turnover *n* (p 66) amount of business that a company does in a period of time measured in terms of the amount of money obtained from customers

U

unauthorised *adj* (p 73) without official permission

underestimate *v* (U13 T22) fail to guess or understand the real cost, size, difficulty, etc. of something and think it is less

underpaid *adj* (p 82) paid less than the market rate

undertaking *n* (p 23) formal promise

undervalue *v* (p 31) consider someone or something as less valuable or important than they really are

unethical *adj* (p 101) not morally acceptable

union (also **trade union**) *n* (p 85) organisation that represents the people who work in a particular industry, protects their rights, and discusses their pay and working conditions with employers

union rep *n* (p 86) worker elected by workers in a factory or business to represent them in discussions with management

up and running *adj* (p 60) operating

update *v* (p 19) give someone the most recent information

V

vacancy *n* (p 25) job that no one is doing and is therefore available for someone new to do

vagaries *pl n* (U19 T9) any of a set of unusual or unexpected events or changes that have an effect on someone

value for money *adj* (p 32) something well worth the money spent

VAT return *n* (p 37) declaration of Value Added Tax (= a type of tax in European countries which is paid by the person who buys goods and services)

venture *n* (p 15) new activity, usually in business, which involves risk or uncertainty

vision *n* (p 10) ability to imagine how a country, society, industry, etc. could develop in the future and to plan in a suitable way

voluntary redundancy scheme *n* (p 91) arrangement when a company needs to reduce its workforce and some employees choose to be made redundant (because they have found another job or would like to stop working)

W

white-collar worker *n* (p 85) person who works in an office or at a professional job, rather than one who works with their hands

within budget *adv* (p 19) not exceeding the amount of money you have available to spend

word of mouth *n* (p 103) people telling each other how good a product is

work out *v* (p 34) calculate

work–life balance *n* (p 85) amount of time you spend at work compared with your free time

workload *n* (p 15) amount of work to be done, especially by a particular person or machine in a period of time

workstation *n* (U20 T10) area in a workplace where one person works

Answer key

Unit 1

Vocabulary
1 1 b 2 g 3 a 4 c 5 e 6 d 7 f
2 1 Getting ahead 2 boils down to
   3 sticking to 4 're/are starting out
   5 talk over 6 come up with 7 turn up
4 1 d 2 c 3 b 4 a 5 h 6 g 7 f
   8 i 9 e
5 1 dress code 2 cut-throat competition
   3 market share 4 rat race
   5 made redundant 6 sink or swim
   7 red tape 8 board of directors
   9 bottom line

Grammar
1 The yardstick (which/that) we use to
   measure our success is customer
   satisfaction.
2 Our production process has been
   undergoing some streamlining, which
   should have a beneficial effect on our
   bottom line.
3 We will be receiving a visit from the
   chairman of the board, whose recent
   email you saw, next week.
4 Our company is situated in a quiet area
   which is right in the heart of the
   country.
5 They've just given me a bonus which is
   the equivalent of three months' salary!
6 In our company, problem-solving takes
   place at informal get-togethers, during
   which everyone sits down on some
   sofas near the coffee machine.
7 Some companies whose corporate
   culture is quite traditional have strict
   dress codes. OR Some companies
   whose dress codes are strict have a
   quite traditional corporate culture.
8 You set me some goals which/that
   were/are impossible to achieve.

Unit 2

Vocabulary
1 1 attention 2 responsibility
   3 appraisal 4 delegation
   5 underlying 6 billionaire 7 success
   8 businesses
2 1 B 2 C 3 A 4 D 5 C 6 B 7 A
   8 D 9 A 10 C
3 1 time-management
   2 quality management
   3 crisis management
   4 brand management
   5 risk management
   6 line management
   7 middle management
4 1 in 2 in 3 on 4 ahead/on
   5 on/to 6 for/with 7 for
   8 in/over/during 9 from 10 under

Grammar
1 Like 2 As 3 As 4 like 5 as
6 as 7 like 8 as

Unit 3

Reading
1 for 2 by/with 3 how 4 As
5 the 6 or 7 take/bring 8 in 9 to
10 which/that 11 other/second
12 latest/earliest/soonest 13 as/for
14 If

Vocabulary
1 1 overworked 2 overpriced
   3 overvalued/(overrated)
   4 overstaffed 5 overestimated
   6 overqualified 7 overfunded
   8 overreacting
2 1 underworked 2 underpriced
   3 undervalued/underrated
   4 understaffed 5 underestimated
   6 underqualified 7 underfunded
   8 underreacting
3 1 overused
   2 overprepared/(underprepared)
   3 oversleeping 4 underrate
   5 overcharged

4 1 c   2 b   3 d   4 e   5 f   6 a
5 1 oversee   2 overbearing
3 overwhelming   4 overdrawn
5 undercut   6 overheads

Unit 4
Vocabulary
1 1 timescale   2 meeting   3 latecomers
4 poor   5 run   6 just   7 miss
8 ahead   9 timing
2 1 h   2 a   3 f   4 d   5 b   6 i   7 c   8 e
9 g
3 1 outline   2 outspoken   3 outset
4 output   5 outlook   6 outselling
7 outperformed   8 outcome
9 outstanding

Reading
1 A   2 C   3 B   4 B   5 D   6 B   7 D   8 B
9 D   10 C

Unit 5
Vocabulary
1 1 assistant, assistance   2 advertisement,
advert, ad, advertiser, advertising
3 reliability, unreliability   4 rely
5 rival   6 rival, unrivalled   7 retainer,
retention, retainment   8 profit
9 profitable, unprofitable   10 strategic
11 satisfaction, dissatisfaction
12 satisfied, dissatisfied, satisfactory,
unsatisfactory   13 loyalty
14 organisation, organiser
15 organised, organisational,
disorganised   16 acquisition, acquirer
17 expansion   18 apologise/apologize
19 apologetic   20 cancellation
2 Possible answers (this list is not
exhaustive): business account,
business manager, business strategy,
buying habits, customer account,
customer care, customer manager,
customer retention, customer services,
human resources, management policies,
management resources, management
strategy, product development, profit
margins, savings account
3 1 buying habits   2 customer retention
3 human resources, business strategy
4 customer care; profit margins

Reading
1 C   2 B   3 D   4 B   5 C   6 A   7 D   8 B
9 A   10 D   11 C   12 D

Unit 6
Vocabulary
1 1 C   2 B   3 A   4 C   5 D   6 B   7 A
8 D   9 A   10 D
2 1 go about   2 go for   3 team up with
4 put together   5 come up with
6 bid for   7 work out   8 come to
3 Across: 3 cover   4 submit   5 business
6 devote
Down: 1 establish   2 assess   3 compete

Grammar
1 hadn't recruited; wouldn't have bought
2 introduced
3 did; would(n't) find
4 could easily have afforded; had budgeted
5 would learn; sent
6 had devoted; would have got(ten)
7 wouldn't bid; thought

Unit 7
Vocabulary
1 1 While   2 in response to
3 in connection with   4 apart from
5 since   6 in turn   7 therefore
8 Apart from   9 and at the same time
10 Furthermore
2 Suggested answers: account holder,
account manager, account number;
company car, company furniture,
company manager, company worker;
computing error, computing
instructions, computing skills; contact
instructions, contact number; entrance
hall; export instructions, export
manager; key error, key holder, key
instructions, key manager, key skills,
key worker; negotiating skills; office
furniture, office holder, office manager,
office number, office worker; operating
error, operating instructions, operating
skills

Grammar
1   The old computer system should have
been replaced three years ago.

2 Nothing was said at the meeting about a change of supplier.
3 The component specifications might need to be revised.
4 No losses have been reported in the last ten months.
5 New government regulations may be brought into effect next year.
6 Funds must have been allocated for this in their budget.
7 This product is being / has been marketed for the first time in the USA. OR This product has not been marketed in the USA before.
8 Simon would never have been recruited if he hadn't been so brilliant at his interview.

Reading
1 ✓   2 one   3 of   4 to   5 after   6 being
7 some   8 ✓   9 more   10 increases
11 doing   12 ✓   13 the   14 open
15 have   16 ✓   17 they   18 ✓   19 ✓
20 up   21 still   22 ✓   23 it   24 for
25 ✓

Unit 8
Vocabulary
1   1 f   2 c   3 h   4 k   5 d   6 i   7 j   8 a
    9 e   10 g   11 b
2   1 allocated   2 per capita   3 shelf life
    4 burgeoning   5 fluctuations
    6 boosted   7 capitalising on
    8 penetration   9 gain ground on
    10 affluence; spending power / spending power; affluence

Writing
Sample answer
Well, I have two main points to make: firstly, if you look at the two charts, **you can see that** the big players, Nestlé and Unilever, have been squeezing the Thai market in a bid to increase their market share. **In terms of** sales, Nestlé has increased its share from 30 to 35 per cent in the last year, while Unilever has maintained its position as market leader without increasing market share; **to be exact**, Unilever's market share has remained at 45 %. **Apparently**, though,

both major brands have increased their sales as a result of advertising.
My second point refers to the other players in the Thai market. As you can imagine, their sales and market share have decreased somewhat, down from 25 per cent to 20 per cent, but, **to give you a bit more background**, I should point out that several of these are niche luxury products rather than mass-market products, and they are unlikely to be worried by Unilever and Nestlé's activities.

Grammar
1 Could you tell me how ~~do~~ you intend to boost sales?
2 I wonder how much **it will** cost to launch our products in the Far East.
3 I **would** be grateful if you could tell me what our projected market penetration is for next year.
4 Can you ~~to~~ tell me how much spending power is forecast to increase in Thailand?
5 Do you happen to know what ~~is~~ the shelf life of our rivals' products **is**?

Unit 9
Vocabulary
1   1 brand building   2 brand awareness
    3 product launch   4 market share
2   1 c   2 d   3 b   4 a   5 e
3   1 C   2 C   3 D   4 D   5 B   6 B   7 A
    8 D

Reading
Suggested answers
1 came   2 what/which   3 most   4 in
5 make   6 likely/known   7 come
8 give/send   9 do   10 during/over/in
11 afterwards/after   12 about/of   13 able
14 how   15 in

Grammar
Suggested answers
1 I'm just writing briefly to report on the effectiveness of the advertising we've been doing recently. / I'm just writing to briefly report / on the effectiveness of the advertising we've recently been doing.

2 Unfortunately, sales have been disappointingly slow, despite our campaign.

3 Frankly, I think this is because the advertisements do not state what we do clearly enough. / Frankly, I think this is because the advertisements do not state clearly enough what we do.

4 They do state that we are electrical engineers. Curiously, however, they don't state what our speciality is, i.e. repairing electric motors.

5 Also, I was looking at the page just an hour ago and I notice that it looks surprisingly similar to advertisements for our rivals, Manning Ltd.

6 Indeed, people quite often phone us up asking if we are Manning Ltd. / Indeed, people phone us up quite often asking if we are Manning Ltd. / Indeed, people phone us up asking if we are Manning Ltd quite often.

7 I firmly believe that we need to continue advertising.

8 However, we need to improve the appearance of our advertisements urgently. / However, we urgently need to improve the appearance of our advertisements.

9 I'm meeting a friend from an advertising agency tomorrow, and hopefully he'll come up with something which works more effectively. / Tomorrow I'm meeting a friend from an advertising agency and hopefully he'll come up with something which works more effectively.

Unit 10
Vocabulary
1 Across: 3 screen out   4 website   7 Banner ads   8 search engine   Down: 1 browser   2 pop-up boxes   5 link   6 online
2 1 makes   2 doing   3 make   4 make   5 doing   6 make   7 make   8 doing

Reading
1 its   2 time   3 ✓   4 it   5 up   6 than   7 was   8 to   9 a   10 ✓   11 just   12 ✓   13 the

Writing
Sample answer
This report summarises the relationship between four supermarkets' market shares and the amount they spent on advertising last year. The supermarket with the largest market share was Freshco with 40% of the market and with an advertising budget of €30 million. They were followed by Cambra with a 28% market share, although their outlay on advertising was higher than Freshco's at €32 million. The supermarket in third place was Quickbuy, who had just 18% of the market, despite spending €28 million on advertising, almost as much as Freshco. Finally, Superday had a 13% market share while spending just €5 million on advertising. The statistics therefore do not show any clear relationship between the amount spent on advertising and the companies' market shares.

Unit 11
Vocabulary
1 1 sales pitch   2 prospect   3 sales volume   4 selling point
2 1 A   2 C   3 D   4 B   5 D   6 C   7 B   8 D

Grammar
1 've been doing   2 haven't seen; Have (you) been working   3 haven't finished; Have (you) been waiting   4 have increased / have been increasing; haven't achieved   5 've been working; 's been; 've sold   6 've been meaning; 've had; haven't managed   7 've been sharing   8 've told   9 've been trying; haven't come   10 's taken; 've taken

Writing
Sample answer
This report summarises the performance of three lines of products: soft drinks, ice-creams and hot snacks, sold by Freshco Supermarkets last year. Sales of soft drinks remained fairly steady for the first two quarters at around $45 to $50 million per month. In July and August however, they soared to $80 million before receding to

$40 million in September and declining still further to $30 million in November. However, they recovered in December to reach $45 million.

Ice-creams sold approximately $10 million per month during the first quarter before rocketing in the months May to August and peaking in August at $120 million. They then plummeted to just $10 million in November and recovered to just over $20 million in December.

Hot snacks sold approximately $100 million per month in the first two months of the year, after which their sales shrank to just under $80 million in April and little more than $60 million in June. They then rose again to $80 million in July before dipping to $60 million in September, after which they soared to reach $120 million in December.

In summary, the figures show that sales of all three lines are highly seasonal.

Unit 12

Vocabulary
1 D   2 A   3 B   4 D   5 B   6 C

Grammar

1 1 Do you mind if I ask you a few questions about your business?
2 First, can you tell me how many employees your company has?
3 Would I be right in thinking that most of your staff come to work by car?
4 And one last question: do your staff have problems parking at work?
5 Would you be interested in leasing parking spaces for your employees?

2 1 The last thing I intend to do is (to) give all the work to you. *OR* give you all the work.
2 What I didn't expect was such a generous bonus.
3 All I said was (that) I was a bit doubtful.
4 It was the low price which really interested me in the product. *OR* It was the product's low price which really interested me. *OR* It was the low price of the product that I was really interested in.

5 All my staff do is complain all day. *OR* All my staff do all day is complain.
6 It was the managing director who was responsible for the mix-up.
7 What they did was (to) outsource all their sales to an outside agency.
8 The last thing (that) we want is a visit from head office.
9 What we need is a completely new sales strategy.
10 All you have to do is (to) sign this form.

Reading
1 Paragraph 1 relates the phone call to what Rosa can offer.
Paragraph 2 explains the service in more detail.
Paragraph 3 tells Mr Slade about other satisfied customers.
Paragraph 4 refers to a meeting arranged for the following Friday.

2 1 time   2 own   3 there   4 where   5 both   6 What   7 All   8 do   9 is   10 take   11 with   12 would   13 with   14 much   15 in

Unit 13

Vocabulary
1 1 talk someone into   2 turned down   3 go about   4 fell short of   5 pay off   6 up-and-coming   7 catch on
2 1 Turnover   2 Depreciation   3 Pre-tax profits   4 Profit and loss for the period   5 Shareholders' equity   6 stock   7 Premises   8 Total fixed assets   9 Goodwill   10 Overdraft

Grammar
1 I'm sure we won't do this, but if we **reduced** our overheads, our cashflow would be much healthier.
2 Our products are really attractive, and if they **catch** on, we'll make a fortune.
3 I wouldn't have managed to talk him into working for me if he **hadn't been** turned down for that job last year.
4 The company would **have gone** bankrupt last year if it hadn't been given an overdraft by the bank at the last minute.

5 If we **don't** lay off 20 % of the workforce, we won't be able to keep our heads above water – it's really necessary that we do so.

6 Redlands wouldn't have introduced a flexible working system if the workers **hadn't** demanded it.

Reading

1 operating profit   2 turnover   3 volume
4 Pre-tax profit   5 net profit
6 fixed assets   7 forecast

Writing

Sample answer
Dear Andrew,
Although our sales were forecast to decrease from €700 million in the first quarter to €500 million in the second quarter, in fact they rose from just under €600 million to €600 million. In the third quarter, they were forecast to rise to €1,000 million but sales performed considerably better and soared to almost €1,400 million before plunging to €300 million in the last quarter, rather less than our forecast of just over €400 million.
Pre-tax profits rose from €100 million in the first quarter to just under €200 million in the second. They then doubled in the third to €400 million before falling back to €100 million in the last quarter.
Please let me know if you require further information.
Best wishes,

Unit 14
Grammar

1 1 Being; having; presenting   2 bringing
3 speaking   4 to put   5 having
6 to start   7 to back; losing   8 to see
9 to make   10 to reduce   11 to be
12 to invest   13 surviving   14 to break

2 1 holding → to hold   2 ✓
3 visiting → to visit   4 ✓
5 knowing → to know   6 phoning →
to phone   7 to buy → buying
8 giving → to give   9 ✓
10 ✓   11 ✓   12 ✓
13 to break → breaking

Reading

1 C   2 A   3 C   4 B   5 A   6 B   7 A   8 D
9 B   10 D   11 D   12 B   13 A   14 D
15 C

Unit 15
Vocabulary

1 1 overtrading   2 overdue   3 overdraft
4 overvalued   5 outgoings   6 outlets
7 upmarket   8 unauthorised   9 undue
10 outcome   11 outlay   12 upfront

2 Suggested answers
bookkeeping skills, cash constraints, cash limit, cash payment, credit limit, credit worthiness, overdue payment, punitive bank charges, root cause, time constraints, time limit, unauthorised overdraft, unauthorised payment, undue pressure

3 1 cash payment   2 bookkeeping skills
3 punitive bank charges; credit limit
4 root cause   5 time constraints
6 unauthorised overdraft
7 undue pressure   8 credit worthiness

Reading

1 Do you remember   2 I put you onto
3 a couple of years back   4 now
5 having   6 getting them to pay   7 if
8 having   9 to the tune of   10 We've told
11 we're not going to   12 anything else
13 we're   14 think of   15 taking them to
court   16 Even talking to them is hard
17 sometimes   18 don't   19 say   20 job
21 isn't available   22 so   23 the whole
thing   24 getting pretty frustrating
25 don't know   26 you're still selling to
them   27 we don't have much   28 sort of
thing   29 deal with   30 for us

Unit 16
Vocabulary

1 not ideal   2 as long as   3 on our list
4 get down to   5 go over   6 jotted down
7 straight; upfront   8 agenda   9 Suppose; discount

Grammar

1 Suppose/Supposing/Imagine 2 on (the one) condition / providing / provided
3 unless 4 unless 5 as long as / provided / providing 6 suppose/supposing/imagine
7 on (the one) condition / provided / providing 8 as long as / providing / provided / on (the one) condition (that)
9 suppose/supposing/imagine
10 Suppose/Supposing/Imagine

Reading

1 arising 2 than 3 were 4 to 5 ✓
6 is 7 are 8 too 9 been 10 a 11 ✓
12 with 13 ✓ 14 would

Writing

Sample answer

Dear Fernando,

Thanks for your email outlining the outcome of staff/management negotiations. There are some points, however, which I think need clarifying. For example, you mention a salary increase 'this year' of 3 %. Please could you clarify exactly what you mean by 'this year'. Does this mean this 'calendar' year (i.e. from January), the company's financial year, or 'a year from now'? Please confirm which. Also, you mention that this will be linked to inflation for the following two years, providing that staff keep to the three-year deal. However, you give no specific details about what this 'three-year deal' is. Please could you list full details of it for me? You mention that flexible starting and finishing times can be agreed with supervisors and managers. However, will there be any limits to this? You don't mention any in your email. For example, will there be a time (e.g. 7.00 a.m.) before which staff cannot commence work (e.g. because the buildings will still be locked) and a time at the end of the day after which they cannot work (e.g. 7.00 p.m.) for the same reason? Are there certain busy times of day when each member of staff must be at work? Please give us these further details. Finally, you talk about productivity rising by 5 %. I would like to know how this will be measured (especially for office staff) and by whom. I'm sure I'm not alone in requiring further information on this. I look forward to hearing from you about all these matters.

Best wishes,

Unit 17

Vocabulary

1 C 2 A 3 B 4 D 5 D 6 D

Grammar

1 1 One 2 He 3 one 4 this 5 there
6 where 7 herself 8 her 9 whose
10 what 11 its 12 those 13 which
14 do 15 such

2 1 I'm director of R&D, and as such, I'm in charge of all new product development.
  2 The date of our next meeting has been postponed, and that/this will mean that no decision will be taken for at least a month.
  3 They were advised to place an advertisement in all major national newspapers, and they did so/which they did.
  4 Monique and Michelle did an MBA together at London University. Now the former works for Tesco and the latter works for Asda, two of the largest supermarket chains in Britain.
  5 Kostas and Dimitriou were our representatives in Greece. Both of them were made redundant when we closed our operation there.
  6 Marcel is the finance director. He is the one who took the decision – and it was a difficult one.
  7 He's asked me to take over the Berlin office and I've agreed to do so.
  8 Sven has been discussing the problem with Franz, but they don't agree with each other.

3 1 Repetitive work often gives rise to boredom and demotivation amongst workers.
  2 Pressure from rivals sometimes causes companies to cut prices.

3 Some late payers have given rise to cashflow problems / the cashflow problems we're having.
4 Delivery problems have arisen as a result of / because of / due to the bad winter weather.
5 Their low productivity led to us/our laying off some workers. / Some workers' low productivity led to us/our laying them off.
6 Workplace accidents are an/the occasional consequence of tiredness.
7 Excessive stress sometimes causes him to lose his temper.
8 Breakdowns in customer relations are a major consequence of over-reliance on computer systems.

Unit 18

Vocabulary

1 1 temp   2 shop-floor   3 union rep
   4 freelancer   5 project manager
   6 white-collar
2 1 c   2 f   3 d   4 b   5 e   6 a
3 1 self-controlled   2 self-employed
   3 self-sufficient   4 self-explanatory
   5 self-financing   6 self-disciplined
4 1 stuck in a rut   2 in the long run
   3 on the go   4 get taken on
   5 the going rate
5 1 underpaid   2 prestigious   3 obsolete
   4 pervasive   5 overwhelming
   6 unprecedented   7 frenetic
   8 booming
6 Suggested answers
   1 as   2 to   3 being
   4 each/both/have   5 to
   6 Although/Though   7 so
   8 which   9 with   10 out   11 if
   12 fell/got/was   13 over   14 met
   15 made

Unit 19

Vocabulary
1 C   2 B   3 D   4 B   5 D   6 C

Grammar
1 1 may have sabotaged   2 must have made   3 can't have broken   4 must be

using / must have been using / must have used   5 might have sent
6 may have spoken / may have been speaking / may be speaking   7 must have read   8 could have got   9 should be making   10 can't have forgotten
2 Suggested answers
   1 be ill. / be taking the day off.
   2 have broken down already. / be malfunctioning already.
   3 have spent it all already.
   4 be really pleased with your performance. / have worked really hard.
   5 have told them they had no chance of winning.
   6 know what he's talking about.

Reading
1 B   2 C   3 A   4 D   5 C   6 D   7 D
8 C   9 C   10 C   11 B   12 A

Unit 20

Vocabulary
1 1 suggest   2 accept   3 thing   4 think
   5 question   6 possibility   7 consult
   8 come back   9 saying   10 acceptable
   11 prepared   12 However
2 1 clock   2 collar   3 mouth   4 passed
   5 scratch/standard   6 neck

Grammar
1 1 f   2 a   3 d   4 e   5 b   6 c
2 Suggested answers
   1 Had my company landed the contract, we'd have undertaken a big expansion programme. / Had I taken more care with the report, it wouldn't have contained so many mistakes.
   2 As long as I work hard, I'll get promoted.
   3 If it weren't for my university tutor, I would not have got this job.
   4 In the event of my being given promotion, I'll celebrate with you.
   5 Providing I don't get interrupted, I should have the proposal finished by Friday.
   6 If my boss were to leave, I'd get her job.

Reading

1 held   2 with   3 following   4 on
5 will/would   6 rather   7 in   8 It   9 on
10 in   11 who   12 case   13 made
14 will/wishes   15 above

Unit 21

Vocabulary

1 He didn't meet his targets, but at least
   he warned us that he wouldn't.
2 Simply put, the capitalist system is the
   most efficient economic system devised
   to date.
3 I merely want to say that it was a badly
   thought-out project.
4 All things considered, his work was a
   surprising success.
5 She was supposedly sending me the
   contract last week.
6 We thought we had an exclusive
   agreement with these suppliers, but we
   discovered that all the while they were
   supplying our competitors as well.
7 We were advised that they were in
   breach of contract and thus we had the
   contract terminated.
8 He may be totally incompetent, but at
   least he's honest.

Grammar

1 a; a; the; the; the   2 a; –   3 the; the; a
4 an; a; –   5 –; –; the   6 The; a; –; –
7 the; a; the   8 the   9 the; the; the; –; a
10 –; an; –; the

Reading

1 C   2 A   3 B   4 D   5 C   6 A   7 B   8 A
9 D   10 D   11 B   12 D   13 B   14 D
15 C

Unit 22

Vocabulary

1 1 f   2 b   3 a   4 d   5 c   6 h   7 g
   8 e
   Used to describe Charles Banks: *hard-
   driving, straight-talking*
2 1 far-sighted   2 two-faced
   3 hard-headed   4 tight-fisted
   5 hard-driving   6 big-headed
   7 straight-talking   8 tight-lipped

3 1 sustained   2 commitment   3 sound
   4 key   5 pursuit   6 synergies
   7 diverse   8 driver   9 complacent
   10 leverage
4 1 b   2 i   3 c   4 a   5 h   6 e   7 d   8 f
   9 g
5 Suggested answers
   1 the takings from the previous day.
   2 the mortgage on our house.
   3 the supermarket, I saw our products
      on the shelves.
   4 we start by giving them a friendly
      phone call.
   5 the low prices to buy as much land
      as you can afford.

Unit 23

Grammar

1 1 As soon as you've finished the
      report, send it to me.
   2 When you're writing the report,
      include statistics. / Include statistics
      when you're writing the report.
   3 You're going to speak to all the sales
      staff when they come to Head Office
      next week. / When all the sales staff
      come to Head Office next week,
      you're going to speak to them.
   4 He won't be so friendly after he is /
      has been promoted to manager next
      week. / After he is / has been
      promoted to manager next week, he
      won't be so friendly.
   5 The offices are going to be
      redecorated while we are taking /
      take our annual holidays. / While
      we are taking / take our annual
      holidays, the offices are going to be
      redecorated.
   6 You'll have to be careful not to
      exceed your expense account when
      you visit / are visiting Berlin next
      month. / When you visit / are
      visiting Berlin next month, you'll
      have to be careful not to exceed your
      expense account.
   7 Visit their website before you write
      to them. / Before you write to them,
      visit their website.

8 We'll change the details after he goes / has gone home. / After he goes / has gone home, we'll change the details.

2 Suggested answers
1 Our company, which is a world leader in the manufacture of marble floor tiles, is based near Cremona, Italy.
2 The tiles, made from top-quality locally produced marble, are exported to many parts of Europe and the Middle East.
3 We are currently investigating the possibility of opening offices in your country, with a view to marketing our products in your region.
4 We are contacting you because we are looking for a local distributor or collaborator with a chain of outlets who would be interested in stocking our products.
5 Our marketing director, Luigi Bossano, will be visiting your area in the near future in order to meet potential distributors.
6 If you are interested in the possibility of working with us, please let us know when it would be convenient for him to visit you.
7 I enclose a brochure and other company literature which will give you a clearer idea of our products and our company.

3 1 The production line was halted because there was an electrical fault.
2 I missed the meeting owing to a mix-up in the dates. / owing to the dates having got mixed up. / owing to the dates getting mixed up.
3 She was able to sort out the problem thanks to Mr Bossano's help. / thanks to Mr Bossano.
4 I'll visit you with samples of our new products whenever it suits you. / is suitable for you.
5 You should come directly to my office when you arrive. / When you arrive, you should come directly to my office.
6 I've visited the new offices being built on the outskirts of the city.

7 Any money spent on advertising is wasted.
8 Please visit Mr Lee while you are visiting Singapore. / while you are in Singapore.
9 The meeting was a failure due to her rude behaviour. / due to her behaving rudely.
10 We won't be going ahead with the project on account of its/the (high) cost.

Reading
1 ~~where~~ which   2 ✓   3 ~~out~~ up
4 ~~that~~ this   5 ~~travel~~ trip   6 ~~Like~~ As   7 ✓
8 ~~advices~~ advice   9 ~~on~~ in   10 ~~for~~ to   11 ✓
12 ~~Similar~~ Similarly   13 ~~has~~ have   14 ✓
15 ~~informations~~ information   16 ✓
17 ~~fruitfully~~ fruitful   18 ~~yourself~~ you
19 ~~since~~ such   20 ✓   21 ~~too~~ also
22 ~~another~~ other   23 ~~enclosed~~ enclose
24 ✓   25 ~~hear~~ hearing

Unit 24
Vocabulary
1 1 trickier   2 trade away
3 unthinkable   4 calamities   5 hands in the till   6 untoward   7 grasp
8 updating   9 create havoc
10 dreadful   11 duped   12 came under scrutiny   13 overnight
14 devastating   15 was … sued
16 got a bad press   17 misdeeds
18 tarnish
2 1 C   2 A   3 D   4 C   5 B   6 C   7 D
8 B   9 A   10 D
3 1 off   2 to   3 for   4 from; to   5 with
6 on; in   7 out   8 about

Grammar
1 Despite spending a lot of time on risk management, he didn't manage to identify the risk which would eventually ruin the company.
2 Surprising as it may seem, companies' reputations may be damaged by their competitors' misdeeds.
3 Even though they are heavily exposed to risk, the company continues to invest in new technology shares.

4 Even if you are (very) risk-averse, it is absolutely essential to make this investment.

5 Whatever decision you make, we will abide by it.

6 However long the project takes, we will make sure of a successful outcome. / However long it takes, we will make sure of a successful outcome to the project.

7 In spite of the difficulties of the investigation, I think we have at last got to the truth.

8 Although he worked here for 30 years, he never progressed beyond a clerical role.